The Income Revolution

The Income Revolution

Joseph Stark

with Peter Sander

Humanix Books

www.humanixbooks.com

Humanix Books
The Income Revolution

Humanix Books, P.O. Box 20989, West Palm Beach, FL 33416, USA
www.humanixbooks.com | info@humanixbooks.com

Library of Congress Cataloging-in-Publication Data is available from the Library of Congress

Cover Design: Paul McCarthy Design
Interior Design: Scribe Inc.

Humanix Books is a division of Humanix Publishing, LLC. Its trademark, consisting of the word "Humanix," is registered in the Patent and Trademark Office and in other countries.

Disclaimer: Annuities are long-term insurance contracts designed for retirement. As a result, there may be fees or penalties for early withdrawals, including surrender charges, and if taken prior to age 59½, withdrawals may be subject to a 10 percent federal additional tax.

We suggest that you consult with your financial adviser, tax adviser, or other financial professional before making any decisions that could impact your tax situation.

Annuity guarantees are backed by the financial strength and claims-paying ability of the issuing insurance company; they are not insured by the FDIC.

A fixed indexed annuity is not a registered security or stock market investment and does not directly participate in any stock or equity investments or index. The applicable index is a factor that in part determines the interest to be credited.

Creditor protection rules vary from state to state, and while IRA annuities are generally protected from creditors, nonqualified annuity contracts may or may not be protected. We do not provide legal advice and recommend that you consult your legal advisor for details on annuity creditor protection in your state.

ISBN: 978-1-63006-066-4 (Hardcover)
ISBN: 978-1-63006-067-1 (E-book)

Printed in the United States of America
10 9 8 7 6 5 4 3 2 1

CONTENTS

INTRODUCTION

The recent Great Recession was devastating.

During and in the aftermath of the 2008–9 Great Recession, we all witnessed a staggering percentage of American wealth vanish into thin air. Estimates by the US Treasury placed the losses in US household wealth somewhere in the 16 *trillion* dollar range.

These losses had devastating effects on families and retirees. Many people at or near retirement were forced to make life-altering decisions, including extending their working years (if work was available), downsizing their homes, and cutting back on their style of living.

More than ever before in my 30-year career in retirement income planning and the insurance industry, I realized that for those who don't have the amount of time necessary to recover from 37 percent losses or more (which is most of us), it's essential to protect at least a certain amount of your assets.

This was something that I had always believed and preached. But watching it unfold before my eyes in a matter of months left an indelible impression and underscored the value of proper retirement income planning. An impression that lasts to this day.

We're Living Longer than Ever

Just 100 years ago, the human life expectancy was about 50 years. So you can see how, in those days, planning for income in retirement may not have been a top priority.

Things sure have changed. For a variety of reasons, including advances in health care and improving lifestyles, we are living longer than ever before.

Today we currently have 38 people living in the United States who are age 110 or older! By the end of this century, there will be 26 million of us (optimistically, I'm including myself) age 100 or older walking the planet. In the near future, what was once an anomaly will become commonplace!

As I'll show later in chapter 3, the trajectory of living longer is quite apparent upon examining a life-expectancy table. The upshot is that today, more than any time in history, locking in income that will last a lifetime—even if you live to be 120—should be a top priority for anyone serious about the quality of their retirement years. With the good news of longevity comes the responsibility of preparing for it.

Retirement: When It Works and When It Doesn't

I'd like to share a tale of two couples.

Our first couple, Mr. and Mrs. Smith, are both within a year of retiring. They've worked hard and saved hard and have accumulated $500,000, part of which is in a company-sponsored 401(k) plan, and the rest is in a personal savings account. Outside of Social Security, they will rely on this sum to fund their retirement years.

As they considered their approaching retirement and how they would fund it, they became concerned about exposing *all* their retirement assets to the volatility of the market. While the market had had its ups and downs inside their 401(k) plan, over several decades in the aggregate, it had served them fairly well.

But now, faced with a short retirement horizon, they became concerned that they wouldn't have enough time to recover from a bad year in the market like they saw in 2008—just before starting to rely on income from their nest egg. They scheduled meetings with their trusted legal and tax advisors as well as with an independent insurance professional.

In the end, the Smiths decided on a strategy that would protect much of their principal from market corrections. Protecting the purchasing power of their principal and keeping pace with inflation was also very important.

Finally, to address longevity risk, they wanted to be sure they had a protected monthly lifetime income stream in place. This income would supplement Social Security, help pay their fixed expenses, and last as long as they both lived. The Smiths purchased annuities with part of their retirement nest egg.

Our second couple, Mr. and Mrs. Martin, are very similar to the Smiths in that they've accumulated $500,000 in their retirement accounts and personal savings. They, too, faced making decisions about how to allocate the money to generate income in order to supplement their Social Security.

The Martins decided on a mixture of financial vehicles that left the bulk of their assets exposed to market volatility. Their choices also overlooked the effects of longevity and longevity risk on their retirement assets if either of the two were to live beyond their average life expectancy.

If the Martins are fortunate, the market will be kind to them. If not, they may not have the number of years necessary to recover from a significant market correction. What's more, drawing down on their assets for income in a down market could compound the problem.

In addition, with no lifetime income stream in place to address longevity risk, they could be faced with changes in lifestyle, downsizing their home, or going back to work (if work is possible, which it may not be at that point in their lives). The Martins approached retirement with no guarantees. That may work—but it may not.

The Income Revolution **(and Why I Wrote the Book)**

These days, a sound retirement income strategy takes into account a variety of risks and variables. While outside of death and taxes there are no absolute certainties, you can increase your odds of having the retirement years of your hopes and dreams. By recognizing and addressing the risks to your nest egg and consulting with the right professionals, you can be confident that you've built a rock-solid strategy.

Yes, there is alarming news out there regarding solvency issues with Social Security, disappearing corporate pensions, and market volatility. Those issues—along with increased longevity, health care costs in retirement, and so forth—should concern all of us.

But it's not all bad news. For those that take the time to do their homework, there are sound solutions to these problems that can put you on the path to the retirement you've worked for and dreamed of.

Here's my main point: Beyond Social Security and defined benefit pensions, it turns out that annuities are the only other financial vehicle that can offer guaranteed lifetime income. For that reason alone, annuities should be considered as an important option when developing a well-rounded retirement income strategy.

But it's true—annuities come in many shapes and sizes, so consult with trusted professionals. You don't want to buy a sports car if a minivan is needed! So we'll learn more throughout this book about the assortment of annuities available and how they fit into your overall retirement strategy.

Who Should Read *The Income Revolution*

The Income Revolution is written for anyone who has an eye on retirement or who is now in retirement. If you have *any* retirement resources—a traditional IRA, a Roth IRA, 401(k), 403(b), 457, or other employer plans; a defined benefit plan (lucky you!); a profit sharing plan; an SEP for the self-employed; or simply money set aside in a savings account for retirement—this book is for you.

The information and strategies discussed herein can apply to anyone who has set aside money for his or her retirement years. Be the Smiths, not the Martins. You'll sleep better at night, both now and in retirement.

Are you ready?

PART 1

THE RETIREMENT CRISIS

Why "Money for Life" Is More Important than Ever

CHAPTER 1

THE RETIREMENT CRISIS

You've been working hard all your life—"busting your butt," as they say. Building your career, perhaps building a family, and hopefully building a financial legacy.

And someday, you'll retire. Receive the golden watch. Pack up your desk, go to your going-away luncheon, and head triumphantly out the door to enjoy the "three *Gs*" of retirement: golf, gossip, and grandkids. With perhaps a bit of travel, crafting, reading, and relaxing thrown in for good measure.

But wait. Your earned income stops at retirement, and it—or most of it, anyway—needs to be replaced by something. Last paycheck, now the first—what?

As more Americans approach retirement, they get curious. How will they pay the bills? How will they provide for the enjoyment retirement can bring? But these days, it's harder than ever to achieve that secure, "rock-solid," worry-free retirement we all strive for.

Retirement, in fact, was once a fairly steady state designed to last forever, particularly if you worked for a big company or a public sector agency with a solid pension plan. Today, companies have thrown the shackles of the *defined benefit* pension—where they take responsibility for earning and providing you that steady payout *forever*—off their backs.

Sadly, these organizations have thrown that responsibility over the wall *to you.* They have transitioned to *defined contribution* plans where the contribution is predefined (and most of it comes from your earnings), and the investments and thus the outcome become your responsibility. Increasing ranks of entrepreneurs have also helped extend this change. Do mom-and-pop businesses have pensions? Nope.

The Retirement Crisis may have started with this transition, but surely it didn't stop there. Fluctuating investment returns can wreak havoc on retirement incomes, as we saw in recent stock market shocks in 2000–2002 and 2008–9. But a number of other factors have turned the placid, pension-based retirement model on its head, creating the "Retirement Crisis."

What is the "Retirement Crisis," you might ask? Put simply, it's a crisis in confidence that any retirement base is safe and solid *over the full course of retirement* for an individual and, importantly, for his or her spouse.

Today, more and more factors and influences create fear, uncertainty, and doubt about (1) whether you can build a sufficient nest egg and (2) whether that nest egg will last through (an ever longer) retirement.

This chapter addresses the many moving parts of the Retirement Crisis. The Crisis is real, but here's the good news: There are solutions, and these solutions will be touched on in this chapter and discussed throughout the book.

Retirement in a Nutshell

Before embarking to describe the Retirement Crisis, it helps to frame just what we mean by "retirement"—financially speaking. Here, a picture helps:

It doesn't take long to realize that this is a basic budgeting model, with "expenses" having to be matched (or preferably, exceeded) by income.

The "resources" on the right half of the chart come from

- entitlements, chiefly Social Security, the venerable government pension for all
- any pension or regular payout beyond Social Security
- savings, which cover the rest—and importantly, any "unplanned" expenses

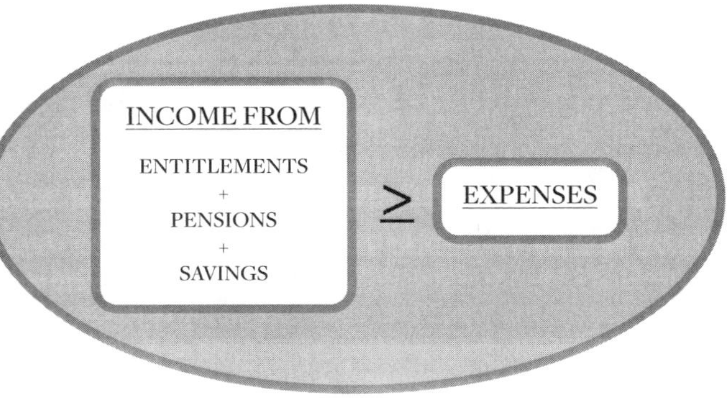

Figure 1.1. The Basic Retirement Planning Model

As we will soon see, the "Retirement Crisis" creeps into every part of this picture. Retiree expenses are rising and becoming less predictable. Social Security is secure for now, but for how long, and how much of the equation does it really provide? Traditional pensions are disappearing, and savings—if you have any at all, and a surprising number of us don't—are challenged more and more by volatile stock markets and low interest rates.

In short, crisis is everywhere.

As we'll see throughout the rest of the book, *annuities*—a pension-like contract that you buy that can last for the rest of your life—are an effective medicine to deal with the crisis when used right.

> Annuities—purchased pension-like contracts that can last for life—are good medicine to combat the Retirement Crisis.

It Costs More: The Relentlessly Increasing Cost to Retire

For a variety of reasons, in an average retirement, we need more money. Routine expenses are higher, unplanned expenses are larger, less is covered by insurance, and it all comes over a longer period as we live longer—and the resources are becoming less reliable than ever before. Talk about a crisis!

Living Better, but for Less?

By the time we approach retirement, we have a pretty good idea of the essential costs of living needed to cover in retirement: food, clothing, home maintenance, basic health care (like over-the-counter medicines), transportation, property/casualty insurance, and so forth. If we've been good budgeters over the years, so much the better.

In retirement, you'll be able to scrap certain costs for commuting, FICA taxes, office clothing, and so on. But here's where the Crisis starts to happen: You'll have a lot more spare time on your hands and want to travel, visit the grandkids, and so forth. More greens fees and more money spent on hobbies drive costs higher. Medicare isn't free. More important, you'll start wanting (or having) to pay others for routine tasks, like home maintenance chores you once did yourself.

Studies still show most people think they can live on 70 to 80 percent of their preretirement income. I happen to think the real number for most is higher, perhaps closer to 90 percent or more.

Health Care Costs: Up and to the Right

Estimates vary, but couples on Medicare spend an estimated $218,000 over the course of a 20-year retirement on deductibles, medicines, and dental care, which are not covered under Medicare. Eye care and hearing aids are also not covered. Costs can rise substantially if the couple is unlucky enough to incur major or persistent expenses related to a chronic disease.

The cost, its unpredictability, and its inevitable rise at rates greater than inflation all contribute to the Crisis.

> Couples at age 65 can expect to spend $218,000 on health care over a 20-year retirement.

Employer-Sponsored Retiree Insurance: Going the Way of the Dinosaurs

The rising cost of health care has forced many companies to drop retiree health coverage or to make it so expensive that it doesn't really help. Only 18 percent of companies recently surveyed provide such coverage, and this figure dropped 25 percent from 2010 to 2014. (If you're employed in the public sector, you have better chances.) Not only is this perk going away, but companies are under no obligation to continue the benefit—you can face the crisis of losing coverage during retirement. Of course Medicare is a good fallback, but . . .

Stretching It Thinner: Rising Longevity

If you're a constant member of the "Life is too short" camp, that's great; you're probably very productive and enjoying yourself being so. However, you may miss the boat when putting together your retirement plan.

Our lives are getting longer and longer. Advances in health care, lifestyle, disease management, and a number of other factors have us now living longer than ever before. Since 2000, our average lifespans have increased 2 years for 65-year-old males (to 86.6) and 2.4 years for 65-year-old females (to 88.8).

Your estimated lifespans are longer the older you are (if you're 80, you're more likely to make it to 90) and the wealthier you are. All these factors add "stretch" to a retirement planning horizon and make it more important to cover the "what-ifs"—what if you live 10 years longer than your planning (and savings) took into account? Life is too long, no?

A crisis will occur for retirement plans based on savings, especially with inflation taken into account. You'll run out of money!

> Since 2000, our average lifespans have increased 2 years for 65-year-old males and 2.4 years for 65-year-old females.

Another Stretch: Early Retirement

When planning for retirement, there's plenty of unexpected to go with the expected. Surely you don't know how long you're going to live. Nobody does. But increasingly, it's harder to know your retirement age. Clearly it depends on you, your health, your resources, and your preferences.

But events entirely out of your control can take charge. What if your company downsizes, putting you out on the street at age 63? For most, it will be hard to land another job and start over; thus early retirement becomes an option. "Early retirement"? Sounds great, doesn't it? Maybe not—if early retirement means you'll have to dig into savings sooner.

Forced early retirement can create a crisis. Be prepared for it.

Family Affairs: You Just Might Have to Care for Someone Else, Too

According to the Employee Benefit Research Institute's (EBRI) 2015 Retirement Confidence Survey, retirees and preretirees age 50 and up now have a 50 percent chance of having to be a caregiver for someone else somewhere along the way, such as a parent or other elderly relative, a sibling, or a child. This is up from 40 percent just a few years ago, likely driven by increased longevity and cost of professional care.

Caregiving can wreak havoc on rock-solid retirement plans, both before and during retirement.

By the way, the EBRI produces an annual study of retirement facts and perceptions based on inputs from both workers and current retirees covering dozens of retirement topics and will be cited throughout the book. See https://www.ebri.org and then search for the study.

Making Ends Meet: The Resources Side

We've covered many, but not all, of the ideas and "gotchas" on the expense side that have caused or fed the Retirement Crisis. But that's not all—ambiguity and change can also fuel the Crisis on the resources side. The following are some things to consider.

Entitlements: Will I Always Be Able to Collect a Social Security Check?

Government entitlements—Social Security, generally speaking—are the most rock-solid part of your resource portfolio. They are guaranteed for life, backed by the government, and indexed for inflation. The problem is, they cover only about 39 percent of our retirement needs, on average. So they represent a great foundation, but other resources must come to fill the gap.

Many question the future viability of Social Security. With current age and payment levels in place, the government trust fund that supports it is expected to be exhausted by 2037—within the horizon for most of you currently planning retirement. As we'll examine in chapter 5, there are fewer workers for every beneficiary, and there are many discussions about changing starting ages and benefit levels.

That said, most don't expect Social Security to disappear, including me. But adjustments will have to be taken into account, especially by younger workers planning to retire.

> Social Security is the best retirement resource ever created. But it covers only 39 percent of the average retirement costs. Younger workers may have to plan for eventual changes.

Pension Suspension: A Great Retirement Solution Going Away

As pointed out in the chapter opening, in an effort to control cost and risks, companies have shifted away from defined benefit pensions, where you get a contracted payout and the company invests the resources and takes the risks to make it happen. Markets drop 40 percent? You still get the same pension.

Pensions are great and almost as good as Social Security. They provide regular income usually to death with surviving spouse benefits. If backed by a solid company or a government agency, they are especially safe, and the Pension Benefit Guaranty Corporation guarantees cover much of the remaining risks. Some are indexed for inflation (mostly government pensions); some are not.

The problem is, only about 18 percent of today's private industry employers offer pensions. Most have switched to defined contribution plans, which are savings plans that shift most of the risk onto the employee.

Pensions are great—if you're lucky enough to have one. Their demise is a main root cause of the Retirement Crisis, for it leaves us exposed to other, more risky retirement resources, like invested savings.

Buying Yourself a Pension: The Annuity "Ticket to Ride"

Don't have a pension? Well, there's good news. You can buy one—it's called an *annuity.* Annuities offer most of the features of the traditional pension, including income for life, spousal protection, and in some cases, inflation adjustments.

With a pension, you get what you get. With an annuity, you can customize it to do exactly what you want—spousal protection, long-term care or death benefits, and direct and indirect linkages with market performance, just to name a few. Figure 1.2 updates the basic retirement planning model to include annuities.

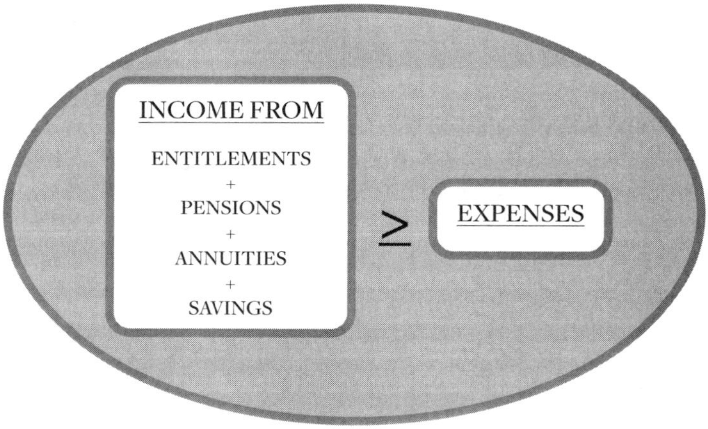

Figure 1.2. Basic Retirement Planning Model, Including Annuities

Savings: Ever More Important, but Ever More Under Fire

As a member of the workforce, you've had it drilled into your head from Day One: *Save for retirement.* Take a few dollars off the top of your paycheck to contribute to a 401(k), 403(b), or some other retirement savings plan. Add some more with traditional or Roth IRAs. You knew it was important to do—now here's why.

Simply put, savings make up the retirement "gap" between available entitlement and pension resources and what you need. They can produce a regular "paycheck" in retirement, and they also cover unexpected and irregular expenses like dental work, hearing aids, and new tires for your car.

The problem is, although savings plans effectively manage and grow your savings, often with a company match of some sort, they can also be subject to the vagaries of the investment markets, in particular the stock market. And if you don't invest in the markets, your returns may not keep up with inflation. What you've saved over the years can take a 20 percent haircut in a single bad year, setting your entire retirement plan on its head.

Pay Up: Here Comes the High Cost of Inflation

Inflation, though quite muted today, plays an important role in the Retirement Crisis. All savings resources are subject to the ravages of inflation. Even at today's moderate inflation rates of 2 percent, a $100,000 savings plan will have only $66,760 in purchasing power at the end of twenty years. The stock market, which rises to a degree with inflation, protects against this somewhat, but it brings risk and volatility with it.

> Even at only 2 percent, inflation can take its toll. A $100,000 investment made today will have only $66,760 in purchasing power in 20 years at a 2 percent inflation rate.

As a consequence, many retirees like to "fix" their savings into a regular, steady payment for life by using at least some of those savings to buy a pension, an annuity. Note that it's a bad idea to convert all savings into an annuity payment—it would be harder to cover unexpected expenses. Also, it is good to maintain at least some exposure to the stock markets. They *do* go up sometimes, and they do counter inflation.

> Savings are subject to the vagaries of the markets. Annuities are a way to convert market investments into a safe, secure life payment.

What's That Interest Rate? 0.1 Percent?

Not too many years after companies started doing away with traditional pensions, a funny thing started happening to monetary policy. Basically, monetary policy governs the amount of money placed in circulation by the Federal Reserve. Once tied to high interest rates to combat rampant inflation—mainly oil price based and mainly in the 1970s—monetary policy started to be deployed to stimulate the economy. Translation: lower interest rates.

In the early 1980s, you could put money in a savings account and earn 5 percent. Some entirely safe money market funds earned as much as 10 percent. Although inflation was higher than it is today, you could make pretty decent and safe retirement returns just by putting money in the bank.

No more. With Federal Reserve benchmark interest rates near zero since the Great Recession in 2008, savings in all forms—from regular savings to CDs to money market funds to safe bonds—return practically nothing, generally not even the inflation rate.

Another "pillar" of the Retirement Crisis is that you have to invest in something risky to get a decent return.

Here again, annuities offer a way to beat low interest rates and to deploy some savings into an investment with relatively safe returns and a guaranteed payout.

Up We Go, Down We Go: The Volatility Roller Coaster

Another danger we can encounter in the dark forests of the Retirement Crisis is the two-headed monster of risk and volatility. The two heads bring angst and instability to your retirement savings. Risk is the possibility that an investment may collapse due to any number of factors internal or external to the investment. Volatility is the up-and-down movement of an investment or market around an average, or a trend line. This is tech talk, but what it means is that your investment can gain or lose value *at any time* due to any number of factors you can't control.

We'll go after volatility a bit more in chapter 6, but as a quick illustration, consider the movement of the S&P 500 broad-based stock index over 20 years, from 1996 through 2015. On average over that period, without dividends, the index gained 7 percent. *Darned good!* you might rightly exclaim.

Yes, darned good. But with a lot of volatility, again as we'll see. In fact, from 2000 through 2015, the average gain was only 3.5 percent—with even more volatility. With bad years like 2002 and 2008 in hindsight, the gain (the reward) may not always be worth the risk!

However, as table 1.1 shows, there's a heck of a lot of variation around this average.

TABLE 1.1. S&P Volatility: 1996–2015

Year-over-Year Gain Not Including Dividends (%)	
1996	+20.3
1997	+31.0
1998	+26.7
1999	+19.5
2000	−10.1
2001	−13.0
2002	−23.4
2003	+26.4
2004	+9.0
2005	+3.0
2006	+13.6
2007	+3.5
2008	−38.5
2009	−8.6
2010	+30.0
2011	+2.0
2012	+14.3
2013	+32.4
2014	+13.7
2015	+1.4

Now, I usually like to show ups and downs as a graph, but here it has more impact as numbers. Remember that placid, friendly 7 percent gain over the period mentioned just now? Well, did you know that over the 20 years, the annual gains or losses ranged from a heady 32.4 percent gain in 2013 down to a disastrous 38.5 percent loss in 2008? Wow. Does any year actually get close to that calm 7 percent? We had 9 percent in 2004, but everything else is simply all over the place.

As I said, "Wow." The crisis isn't the gain or loss—in fact, we've gained (whether we will continue to do so is another question)—it's the volatility that can grind up a retirement plan. Those who planned to retire in 2008 found out the hard way.

Summing Up: A Crisis for All of Us

- Nobody can avoid the Retirement Crisis. Increasing life expectancy, rising costs, and less dependable retirement resources will get us sooner or later.
- A rock-solid retirement is still possible, it is just harder to attain with traditional resources and more likely to fail due to the unforeseen.
- Elements of the Retirement Crisis include
    - higher living costs and standards of living
    - increased life expectancy
    - higher health care costs
    - little to no employer-sponsored retiree health insurance
    - forced earlier retirements
    - caregiver obligations
    - Social Security concerns
    - disappearing pensions
    - inflation
    - miniscule interest rates on savings
    - market volatility

- You can't build a retirement plan that's completely rock solid, but you can make at least some parts of your retirement plan more solid and dependable.
- There *are* solutions to the Retirement Crisis. Many seek to counter the unknowns of the Crisis by combatting the unknowns of longevity and market performance with annuities.

We want more out of retirement. We want it sooner. We want it to last longer. Rock-solid components, like entitlements and pensions, are covering an ever decreasing portion of the bill. Savings are exposed to market volatility and miniscule interest rates.

We need and want more on an ever shakier foundation.

It's a crisis.

Annuities won't solve everything, but they will help.

CHAPTER 2

THE BIG "WHEN"

The Challenge of Increased Longevity

You just got home from helping your 95-year-old mother-in-law with her grocery shopping. She's lively, talkative, and active, but you really had to do most of the work and help with most of the decisions. As you discussed how much the groceries cost, it became pretty clear that she couldn't comprehend what you really meant by "Just a little over $60." And you're pretty sure she wouldn't be able to discuss her current finances and whether they covered the bill.

As spry and perky as your mother-in-law might be, you begin to think about what happens as *you* get older. Will you have enough resources to live as you spend down your savings? Will you even be able to comprehend your exact financial situation? Will you be able to afford retirement? Will you even *know* at the time whether you can?

It all brings up a huge question, one central to the Retirement Crisis and central to retirement planning as well: Just when, exactly, will you finally kick the bucket? How much retirement will you have to cover before that happens?

Consider a few facts:

- In just 13 years since 2000, average life expectancies have grown about 2 years. The average lifespan for a 65-year-old male grew from 81 to 86.6 years. For women who reached 65, it grew from 84 to 88.8 years. (Note that these figures differ from the longevity figures introduced in chapter 1; those figures were for individuals who had already reached age 65. More detail to come later in this chapter.)

- By 2050, the US government projects life expectancy for those already reaching 65 to rise to 83–86 years for men and 89–94 years for women.
- Some 72,000 Americans are age 100 or older, and that number is expected to rise to about 500,000 by the year 2100.

Thanks to advances in medicine and lifestyle, life-spans are getting longer for everyone. So the big question is this: What does that mean for your retirement security? How do you plan for longer average life expectancies, and if you're "lucky" enough to live longer than the averages, how do you guarantee that you won't outlive your money?

Why Living Longer?

Life expectancies have increased from about 35 to 40 years about two centuries ago to about twice that now. That reflects many basic advances in prevention and treatment of disease, trauma, childbirth death, and other killers.

That's all well and good but not of particular interest to those of us planning for retirement.

When a year of retirement costs perhaps $50,000 depending on lifestyle, even a one- or two-year growth in average life expectancies is significant. Over the next 35 years, we might get another 3 to 5 years out of our tired, aching bodies. And as noted above, far greater numbers of us are "superannuating" to ripe old ages exceeding 100.

There are many reasons—and many arguments about what these reasons are—for increased longevity. They boil down to better health and health care, including better technology, vaccinations, improved provision of public health services, better education, and better nutrition.

In the past century, large gains came from the simple provision of clean drinking water. Universal sewage and better personal hygiene entered the race. Then came vaccinations, antibiotics, and better nutrition, especially in the infant and childhood years. Better trauma care and improved drugs came along more recently.

Longevity will continue to be driven higher by more advanced, technology-based health care, with advanced diagnostics, medications, and surgical procedures. These "hard" solutions combine with the softer factors of fitness, better nutrition, and better health consciousness to create an environment where longevity could increase for quite some time—at least through 2050, according to US government studies, and likely for years after that.

Although it has a much greater effect in the Third World, where incomes are much lower, there is some evidence, too, that affluence and prosperity lead to longer lives.

Lengthening life expectancies create special retirement planning needs. You need more money, you may need more long-term care, and—importantly—you need more protection against *outliving* your money. If you're 99 years old and broke, there isn't a whole lot you can do about it!

> Life expectancies are increasing.
>
> You and your spouse are both more likely to live longer.
>
> Annuities are a first-line defense against outliving your money.

Living Longer: By the Numbers

So how much longer are people living these days?

From the Centers for Disease Control US Health Report from 2014, we get figure 2.1. The figure shows the "base case": the life expectancies of males, females, and the two combined from birth.

Several facts jump out:

- Life expectancies have risen considerably since 1900, with combined sex expectancy up more than 30 years since that time (47.3 years in 1900 to 78.8 years in 2013).
- Although the rate has slowed, life expectancy continues to grow gradually.

Specified ages and year	*All races*		
	Both sexes	*Male*	*Females*
At birth			
1900	47.3	46.3	48.3
1950	68.2	65.6	71.1
1960	69.7	66.6	73.1
1970	70.8	67.1	74.7
1980	73.7	70.0	77.4
1990	75.4	71.8	78.8
1995	75.8	72.5	78.9
2000	76.8	74.1	79.3
2001	77.0	74.3	79.5
2002	77.0	74.4	79.6
2005	77.6	75.0	80.1
2006	77.8	75.2	80.3
2007	78.1	75.5	80.6
2008	78.2	75.6	80.6
2009	78.5	76.0	80.9
2010	78.7	76.2	81.0
2011	78.7	76.3	81.1
2012	78.8	76.4	81.2
2013	78.8	76.4	81.2

Figure 2.1. Life Expectancy Starting from Birth

US Centers for Disease Control and Prevention

- Women still outlive men, but the gap is getting slightly smaller; the life expectancy for men is slightly higher.
- Life expectancies have grown by roughly two years since the year 2000.

This from-birth base case is useful, but it helps fine-tune retirement planning by looking at life expectancy for people who reach retirement age, as happens next.

The Older You Get, the Older You Get

It's important to understand overall life expectancy from birth, but if you're unlucky enough to die before retirement, your retirement plan doesn't much matter. However, if you make it to 65, your chances of living to 75 are better because you've successfully navigated the first 65 years. It's more important to understand longevity from your retirement age—that's what you really have to plan for.

Trends in Longevity: Early Stage Retirement

Since you're developing a retirement plan for age 65 (or something close) and beyond, this is the best resource to use to understand how longevity has increased for *new* retirees. Figure 2.2 shows the extension of life likely beyond age 65.

As the figure shows, life expectancy for men has risen more than five years since 1950 and almost two years since 2000 (through 2013). As with longevity from birth, you can see the slow, steady

	All races		
Specified ages and year	*Both sexes*	*Male*	*Females*
At 65 years			
1950	13.9	12.8	15.0
1960	14.3	12.8	15.8
1970	15.2	13.1	17.0
1980	16.4	14.1	18.3
1990	17.2	15.1	18.9
1995	17.4	15.6	18.9
2000	17.6	16.0	19.0
2001	17.9	16.2	19.2
2002	17.9	16.3	19.2
2005	18.4	16.9	19.6
2006	18.7	17.2	19.9
2007	18.8	17.4	20.0
2008	18.8	17.4	20.0
2009	19.1	17.7	20.3
2010	19.1	17.7	20.3
2011	19.2	17.8	20.3
2012	19.3	17.9	20.5
2013	19.3	17.9	20.5

Figure 2.2. Life Expectancy Starting from Age 65

US Centers for Disease Control and Prevention

rise over the years. Of course, you add these figures to "65" to get the final projected ending age.

Trends in Longevity: Late-Stage Retirement

Late-stage retirement planning usually starts at age 75—if you're 75, how much longer will you live, and how fast is this life expectancy growing? You can also see from figure 2.3 a slow, steady increase in life expectancy over the years.

Note that life expectancies for older men and women appear to be growing at a faster rate. For men, expectancies grew by one year over the 20 years from 1980 to 2000. They grew another year in the 10 years following that, an apparent acceleration in longevity for this older age group. Women exhibited a slightly stronger acceleration in longevity—up 0.3 years for 20 years 1980–2000; up another 0.9 years for the 10 years following through 2010.

	All races		
Specified ages and year	*Both sexes*	*Male*	*Females*
At 65 years			
1980	10.4	8.8	11.5
1990	10.9	9.4	12.0
1995	11.0	9.7	11.9
2000	11.0	9.8	11.8
2001	11.2	9.9	12.0
2002	11.2	10.0	12.0
2005	11.5	10.4	12.3
2006	11.7	10.6	12.5
2007	11.9	10.7	12.6
2008	11.8	10.7	12.6
2009	12.1	11.0	12.9
2010	12.1	11.0	12.9
2011	12.1	11.1	12.9
2012	12.2	11.2	12.9
2013	12.2	11.2	12.9

Figure 2.3. Life Expectancy Starting from Age 75

US Centers for Disease Control and Prevention

Understanding *Your* Life Expectancy

The Centers for Disease Control (CDC) tables are helpful, but the Social Security Administration (SSA) also provides a tool, based on much the same data, to estimate your own (and your spouse's) life expectancy in real time.

The life expectancy calculator shown in Figures 2.4 and 2.5 is simple and easy to use and can be found at https://www.socialsecurity.gov/OACT/population/longevity.html.

The result is presented as a breakdown of your life expectancy from your current age, from age 65, from your full retirement age (66 years, 4 months in this example), and from age 70, as shown in figure 2.5.

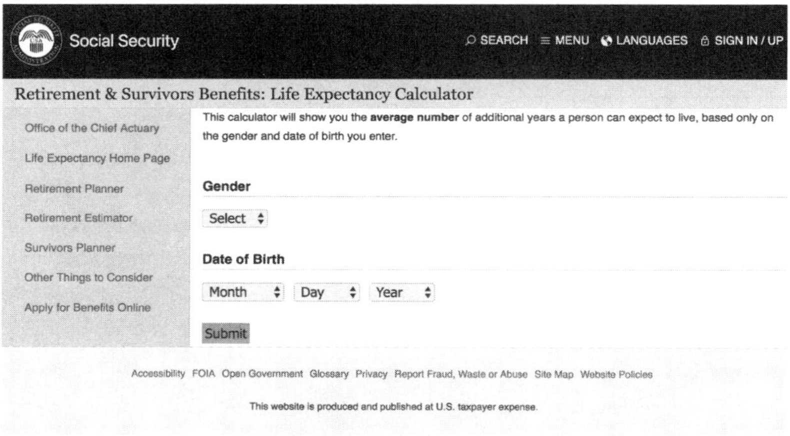

Figure 2.4. SSA Life Expectancy Calculator Main Screen

How to Deal with Living Longer

Longer life expectancies mean, among other things, that you have more years in retirement to cover and plan for. For people expecting to retire in the 2015–20 time period, life-spans have risen a couple of years since many of you made your retirement plans, and they are on track to rise another year or two during the next decade. Three to four years of extra expenses, times two for you and your spouse, can drain considerably more of your resources.

Late-stage retirees likely spend less on housing, food, and most consumer goods but more on health care and significantly more on long-term care, home health, and so forth.

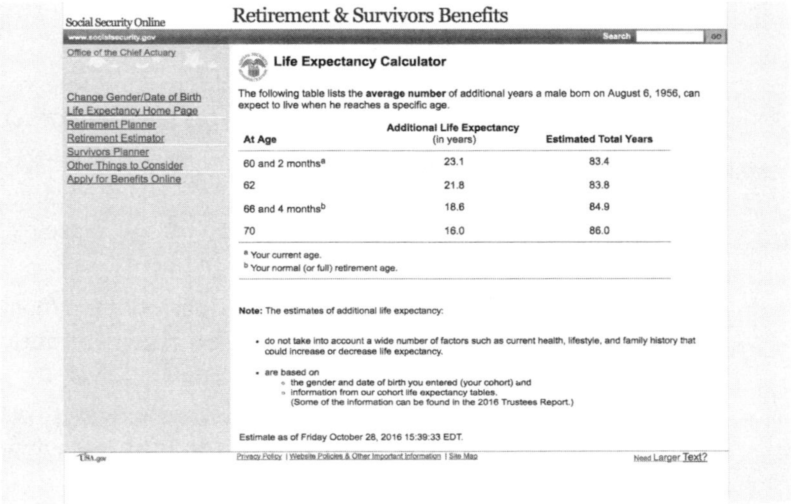
Social Security Online

Retirement & Survivors Benefits

www.socialsecurity.gov

Search GO

Office of the Chief Actuary

Change Gender/Date of Birth
Life Expectancy Home Page
Retirement Planner
Retirement Estimator
Survivors Planner
Other Things to Consider
Apply for Benefits Online

Life Expectancy Calculator

The following table lists the **average number** of additional years a male born on August 6, 1956, can expect to live when he reaches a specific age.

At Age	Additional Life Expectancy (in years)	Estimated Total Years
60 and 2 months[a]	23.1	83.4
62	21.8	83.8
66 and 4 months[b]	18.6	84.9
70	16.0	86.0

[a] Your current age.
[b] Your normal (or full) retirement age.

Note: The estimates of additional life expectancy:

- do not take into account a wide number of factors such as current health, lifestyle, and family history that could increase or decrease life expectancy.
- are based on
  - the gender and date of birth you entered (your cohort) and
  - information from our cohort life expectancy tables. (Some of the information can be found in the 2016 Trustees Report.)

Estimate as of Friday October 28, 2016 15:39:33 EDT.

USA.gov

Privacy Policy | Website Policies & Other Important Information | Site Map

Need Larger Text?

Figure 2.5. SSA Life Expectancy Calculator Results Page

So planning for the last few years of your life can be pretty tricky. Social Security—and again, annuities—take care of this need to a degree. How? By at least covering the *extension* of your life due to longevity, if not the *expansion* of your expenses. Some annuities contain *riders*—special customizable provisions purchased at the beginning—to cover long-term care expenses way down the road.

> Annuities cover the extension of life and sometimes the expansion of expenses in late life.
>
> Again, annuities are a first-line defense against outliving your money.

Summing Up: Longevity Is Increasing and You Need to Deal with It

- The reasons for increased longevity boil down to better health and health care.
- For people expecting to retire in the 2015–20 time period, life-spans have risen a couple of years since many of you

made your retirement plans, and they are on track to rise another year or two during the next decade.

- Life expectancies for people age 75 and older (late-stage retirees) appear to be getting longer at a faster rate than other age groups.
- Not only are average life-spans increasing, but populations in very high age brackets (more than 100 years old) are expected to rise sevenfold throughout the 21st century.
- Late-stage retirees likely spend less on housing, food, and most consumer goods but more on health care and significantly more on long-term care, home health, and similar services.
- For planning purposes, you can estimate your longevity on the SSA's online Life Expectancy Calculator at https://www.socialsecurity.gov/OACT/population/longevity.html.
- Annuities can make your retirement plan more "rock solid" against the risk of longevity.

By the Numbers

- **30.** The approximate number of years that life expectancies have increased since 1900
- **2.** The approximate number of years that life expectancies have increased since 2000
- **89 to 94.** The estimated average life expectancy for women already 65 by 2050—up about 5 years from today
- **500,000.** The expected population over 100, up from 72,000 in 2013
- **0.3 years.** The average increase in life expectancies for women in 1980–2000
- **0.9 years.** The average increase in life expectancies for women in 2000–10

The increase in life expectancies appears to be accelerating.

CHAPTER 3

ARE YOU KEEPING UP WITH THE JONESES?

Thinking about retirement? Thinking about how much you'll need and how much to save? One good place to start is to know how much others just like you need and how much they manage to save.

Consider some facts from the Federal Reserve Survey of Consumer Finances and elsewhere:

- The median household income for active working families is $54,000.
- For US individuals, the average amount saved for retirement is just over $42,000—not even enough to get one "median" US household through one year!
- A third of all workers have not saved anything at all for retirement.
- Households that *do* save average about $104,000 at age 55 and beyond.

Talk about a Retirement Crisis! No savings for so many? Savings of less than a year's worth of expenses for a large number of others? Two years' worth of savings for those who *do* save? Wow.

These figures tell us a lot. They tell us that most Americans still rely on Social Security and the few pensions left to get by. They tell us that most of us are a long way from buying the guaranteed income for a rock-solid retirement through an annuity or similar investment.

The dimensions and causes of the Crisis were put on display in chapter 1. Eventually we'll get to calculating how much *you'll* need to retire based on *your* individual expenses and resources, but before that, it's worth looking at how you stack up against everyone else out there. Are you on track? Behind? Or even ahead of the game?

Your nest egg is for you, not anyone else. But knowing where other people like you stand is a good place to start. You should know how much savings others like you have achieved. Call it peer pressure if you want, but it works!

This chapter offers some enlightening benchmarks to help you see where you are—and hopefully to see where you're going as well.

> People naturally like to "keep up with the Joneses" on homes, cars, phones, boats, and the like. Why not do the same for retirement savings?

First Question: Are You Saving for Retirement at All?

Do you save for retirement? Hopefully the answer is a resounding "yes" if you're of working age. I suspect that if you're reading this book, you probably are—that's a good thing. In a moment, we'll get to whether you're saving *enough*.

As figure 3.1 shows, the percentage of the workforce saving for retirement has hovered in the low 60s—slightly less than two-thirds of the workforce—for quite some time. The figure shows a sag during the Great Recession years starting in 2010, but percentages have recently returned to previous levels against the backdrop of an improving economy.

For most of you, I suspect, we can check this box and move on to looking at how much you save compared to your peers.

You're in Your 50s: Have You Saved Enough?

The longer you work, the more you save, and the more your savings grow. That's the theory, at least.

Workers Saving Money for Retirement

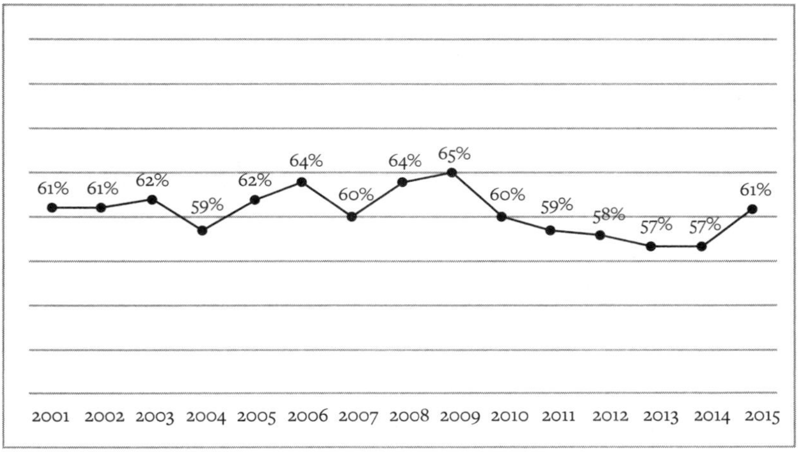

Figure 3.1. Percentage of Workers Saving for Retirement

Source: Employee Benefit Research Institute 2015 Retirement Confidence Surveys

Why? Because income rises (for most people, anyway) and investment returns "compound"—that is, the returns earn returns, a snowball effect we never want to get in the way of. And if you've saved in the right places, that compounding pulls your sled forward ever faster without encountering the drag of taxation.

You'll see lots of "mean" and "median" figures for retirement savings, like the ones I showed at the chapter outset. Where it really starts to get interesting is when we examine savings by age group. If you're 58, quite obviously, you need to have more socked away than if you're 35. Figure 3.2, from Transamerica's 2015 Annual Retirement Survey, shows just how much people have socked away by age group.

The numbers are pretty self-explanatory; if you're in your 60s and don't have $172,000 or more socked away in retirement savings, you're behind the curve.

Note that at this level of savings, you're starting to accumulate enough to consider buying annuities to achieve guaranteed income for life. A $100,000 immediate annuity could return somewhere around $500 a month or more for life (as of early 2016) for a 65-year-old male living in Florida.

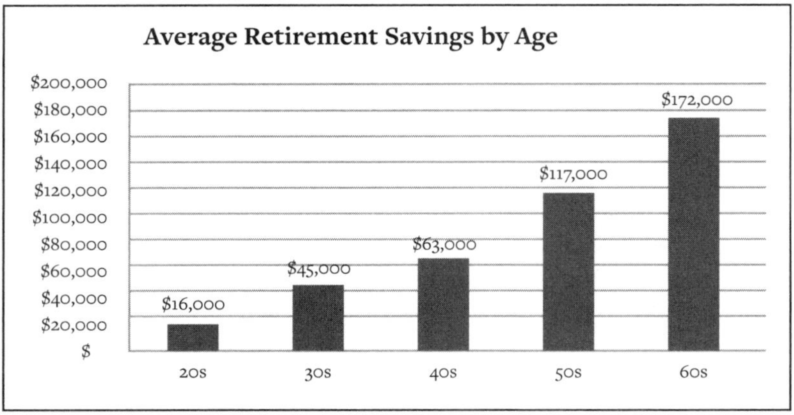

Figure 3.2. Average Retirement Savings by Age

From Transamerica 2015 Annual Retirement Survey

> Your peers have $172,000 in retirement savings by the time they reach their 60s. This is enough to consider buying annuities for lifetime income protection.

Another Look, This Time with Detail: How Much Have Your Peers Saved?

The Transamerica study gives you an important look at how much folks in your age group have saved. Another look, provided by the Employee Benefit Research Institute (EBRI), gives more detail around those averages I mentioned earlier. How many people have saved how much, and how has this changed over the years?

Table 3.1 gives the breakdown.

This breakdown shows some rather eye-catching facts:

- Of those who have saved, 27 to 36 percent have saved less than $1,000.
- That figure hasn't improved much over the 11-year period.
- Retirement savings exhibit a mild "barbell" pattern—the low end and high end are larger than the middle. We have super savers and lightweight savers—not so much in between.

TABLE 3.1. Total Savings and Investments Reported by Workers Providing Response

	2004	2010	2011	2012	2013	2014	2015
Less than $1,000 (%)	↑	27%	28%	30%	28%	36%	28%
$1,000–$9,999 (%)	54	18	17	18	18	18	17
$10,000–$24,999 (%)	↓	11	10	12	12	8	12
$25,000–$49,999 (%)	14	12	11	10	9	9	9
$50,000–$99,999 (%)	11	11	9	10	10	9	10
$100,000–$249,999 (%)	13	11	14	11	12	11	10
$250,000 + (%)	9	11	10	10	12	11	14

Source: Employee Benefit Research Institute 2015 Retirement Confidence Surveys

- The number of savers with more than $250,000 has grown steadily, and more steadily than the other groups.
- If you have $250,000 saved, you're ahead of 85 to 90 percent of your class. Congratulations!

> Twenty-eight percent of saving workers have less than $1,000 saved.
>
> If you have $250,000 saved, you're ahead of 86 percent of your class.

The "Savings Factor": What Should Your Age Group Save, Anyhow?

You've seen where you stand against the "haves" and "have-nots" in the first two sections. Maybe you're feeling good about yourself and your situation, maybe not. The next study, from Fidelity

Investments, shows how much you're likely to *need* in retirement as a function of your projected age-65 income, described as a "Savings Factor."

Fidelity has made some calculations based on your income level (a proxy for lifestyle), savings patterns, investment returns, and withdrawal strategies to arrive at a multiple of your income needed to retire successfully. If you're age 50 and expecting a "normal" retirement, you should have six times your salary saved. It is interesting to observe how the multiple grows more rapidly over time, reflecting the expectation of compounded returns. Also interesting is the bracketed range of "below average, average, and above average" levels giving definition of how far behind or ahead you are.

> You should have eight times your projected age-65 income set aside for a comfortably average retirement.

Got Enough? How Do "Average" Savings Stack Up Against Need?

Figure 3.2, from the Transamerica Study, showed us how much we've saved by age group. Table 3.2 showed us how much Fidelity thinks we should have saved to achieve a level of retirement in line with our projected age-65 income. Do these numbers match?

Wish it were so, but it isn't. As figure 3.3 shows, the average savings by age group falls well short of the Fidelity "Savings Factor" assessment of needs.

For people in their 60s, for example, the Transamerica average saved of $172,000 falls well short of the $540,000 Fidelity suggests you need based on income averaging the median household income at age 67. That falls an incredible two-thirds short. Retirement Crisis, we have bumped into you once again!

TABLE 3.2. The Savings Factor

By Age	Below Average	Average	Above Average
30	1×	1×	1×
35	1×	2×	2×
40	2×	3×	4×
45	3×	4×	5×
50	5×	6×	7×
55	6×	7×	9×
60	7×	8×	10×
67	8×	10×	12×

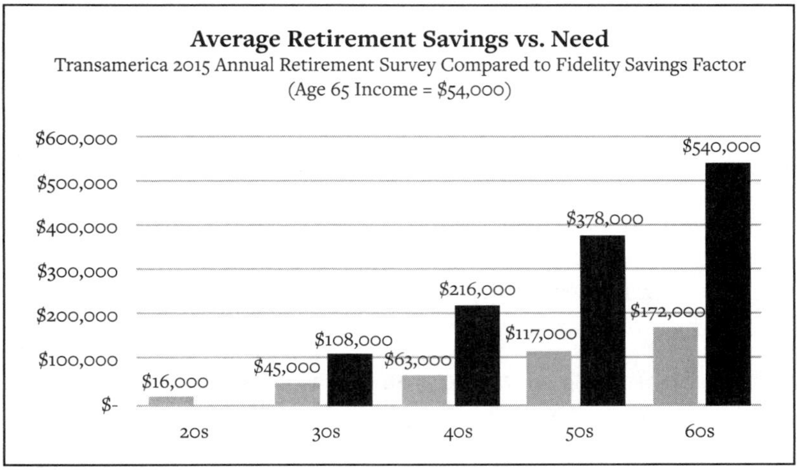

Figure 3.3. Average Retirement Savings Versus Need

Source: Fidelity Investments

Do You Own Your Home?

How do you get relief from the shortfall just described? Do you really need $540,000 on Retirement Day One? Say it isn't so.

A lot of it has to do with lifestyle. It goes almost without saying: The retirement you can afford has a lot to do with your lifestyle and the expenses tied to that lifestyle. A lot also has to do with whether you own your own home. That's one of the big drivers of your expenses, both before and during retirement. Are you still paying for—or paying on—a home?

According to the 2013 Federal Reserve Survey of Consumer Finances, for households age 55 and over,

- 35 percent own a home with no debt
- 24 percent own a home with some debt
- 41 percent do not own a home

I don't make much of line-by-line comparisons of your expenses with your peers, but the home is a biggie. Burn that mortgage and live free and clear and you won't need so much in other resources to retire. And your "Savings Factor" will be substantially lower (although Fidelity provides no insight as to how much lower).

It's a great way to get ahead of two-thirds of the Joneses.

We will do a more customized assessment of your retirement needs and how they match your resources in chapters 11 and 12. We move away from benchmarks to start building your own customized retirement plan in the next chapter.

Summing Up: Peer Comparison Is a Good Starting Point Toward a Rock-Solid Retirement

- The average worker has less than one year's median household income saved for retirement.
- The average worker *who saves* has about two years' worth saved—$104,000.
- A bit less than two-thirds of all workers save for retirement.
- Average retirement savings grow by age group, reaching $172,000 for individuals in their 60s. Because of increasing

incomes and compounded investment returns, savings grow at an accelerating rate.

- The $172,000 savings figure still falls short of the $540,000 Fidelity suggests you need for a normal retirement based on their "Savings Factor."
- Individual savings vary widely around the averages, with 27 percent of workers owning less than $1,000 in savings and 14 percent having more than $250,000. The distribution is sort of a "barbell"—heavy with low and high savers with relatively few in between.
- Whether you own your own home makes a big difference in what you need to save.
- If you follow the "Savings Factor" recommendations, you should have enough to purchase annuities to provide guaranteed income for life.

By the Numbers

- **38.** The percentage of workers who do not save for retirement at all (2015)
- **28.** The percentage of saving workers who have less than $1,000 saved
- **86.** If you have $250,000 saved, you're ahead of 86 percent of your class
- **$172,000.** What the average worker has saved for retirement by his or her 60s
- **$540,000.** What Fidelity suggests the average worker *needs* at retirement (age 67, actually) based on their "Savings Factor" and a salary equaling the median household income
- **35.** The percentage of people who own their own homes at retirement

CHAPTER 4

WHAT'S THE RETIREMENT PLAN, MAN?

So we know there's a Retirement Crisis out there. We know where we currently stand against our brethren when it comes to planning for retirement. But do we have a plan with a retirement destination in mind? A proper road map of what needs to be done to get there?

Most of us have thought about retirement but haven't gone as far as to sit down and put together a retirement plan. As we'll see, only 15 percent of workers have a formal, documented retirement plan. Sure, you can save like crazy, and if you do so, you might luck out and actually have enough. But that doesn't answer all the financial questions—and it answers *none* of the nonfinancial ones.

If your spouse outlives you, how will he or she get by? Will you have enough to support your current home and lifestyle or will you want to downsize? How will you cover health or long-term care? Will you want to or have to work to get by? What happens if you live 10 years longer than your projected life expectancy?

A good retirement plan addresses all these issues—and dozens more. It leads to timed actions, such as purchasing deferred annuities 10 years before retirement, or saving X dollars over Y years to build a nest egg, or paying off your house so the roof over your head becomes an asset, not a liability.

As Yogi Berra once said, "If you don't know where you're going, you won't get there."

What Is a Retirement Plan and Where Do You Get One?

When you started out with your first employer, I'll bet someone from Human Resources contacted you about setting up a "retirement plan." Sure, set up a 401(k) or 403(b), make contributions to it "off the top" of your paycheck, maximize company match, and choose a few investment vehicles. Very well, check the box, done. You have a retirement plan.

Not so fast. Yes, this "retirement plan" does provide a good way to accumulate funds, tax-deferred, for retirement. When you're in your 20s, this is probably enough. Save and figure out the rest later.

But as time goes on, your needs in retirement become more complex and more imminent. Where will you live? How will you cover longevity? What about your spouse? Taxes? Health care? How much will it all cost? How much will be covered by Social Security and, if you're lucky, that pension? Will ends meet? What about a reserve for unplanned expenses?

Simply put, a retirement plan is a deliberate exercise in modeling the future, first in lifestyle, then in dollars. A good retirement plan declares where you will live, how you will live, and what *expected* expenses will arise from the result—with a reserve for the *un*expected. The financial part of the retirement plan puts numbers on all of that.

You can do a retirement plan by simply sitting down with the family, making lifestyle choices, and putting some numbers on those choices. A pad of paper and a spreadsheet will suffice.

The plan covers your expenses and resources, which in turn include entitlements, pensions, and savings (see figure 1.1). Importantly, these items are planned over time—a time period of your choosing. The longer a time period you choose, the greater chance you have to get through with a "rock-solid" retirement. You can hire out this chore to a professional—often a good idea to get the value of experience and fresh perspective on you prospects.

So You Think You're Prepared for Retirement?

Human behavior and emotion can bring some interesting results when it comes to perceptions and realities of retirement planning.

Despite the Retirement Crisis and the recent Great Recession, a surprisingly high (in my opinion) percentage of US workers and current retirees are either "very" or "somewhat" confident in their financial preparation for retirement, which includes planning and actual asset accumulation.

As shown in table 4.1, according to the Employment Benefit Research Institute's (EBRI) 2015 survey, some 68 percent of workers are either "very confident" or "somewhat confident" in their retirement preparation.

TABLE 4.1. Confidence in Financial Preparation for Retirement

Confidence	Workers (%)	Retirees (%)
Very confident	25	37
Somewhat confident	43	37
Not too confident	24	10
Not at all confident	14	14

Source: Employment Benefit Research Institute, 2015

I haven't seen these retirement plans, but I wonder what they really mean by "prepared," and I wonder what it means to be "confident." People living in homes with massive termite infestations often go through life confidently believing nothing is wrong until the roof collapses.

Consider this: According to the same survey, 64 percent of individuals say they're "a little behind schedule" or "a lot behind schedule" when it comes to planning for retirement. So the message here is "confident" but also "behind in planning and saving."

I sense a lot of termites out there.

Not Just the Financial Stuff

Just who do you think you'll be in retirement? The answer to that goes a long way toward developing a useable plan.

Central to the idea of developing a financial retirement plan is building a good working vision of your expected lifestyle. It's your own personal "movie" of who you're going to be, where and how you're going to live, how much you'll travel, what kind of motor vehicles you'll have, what kinds of special considerations—like health needs, supporting grown kids—you'll need to account for, and whether you'll work or not. These factors can really influence the numbers.

As with the numbers themselves, it's good to envision multiple scenarios. You don't know what's going to happen with your health, your living situation, and so forth. It's not a bad idea to plan a "high," "medium," and "low" set of scenarios. It may be a good idea to review your scenarios with a friend or relative to see if *they* envision your retirement lifestyle the way you do.

The Five (Emotional) Stages of Retirement

Gerontologist and researcher Dr. Robert C. Atchley has given us oft-cited research outlining the "Five Stages of Retirement" we all go through as we transition from our workforce roles to become fully engaged and supported in retirement. (Sometimes these are listed as six or seven stages; I'll keep it simple.) I call them "emotional" stages because they often have more to do with your state of mind than actual physical and financial stages, but they can affect a retirement plan and should be considered. The five stages are the following:

1. *Preretirement.* This stage includes disengagement from work, budget preparation, discussion of retirement with spouse and family, planning the timing, and planning the transition.
2. *Honeymoon.* You're out the door! You can sleep late, build birdfeeders, play golf—anything you want! Freedom! Watch out, though, this period can be very short if you're bored or the money situation makes you nervous—say, if the

market tanks 20 percent during your first two months of retirement.

3. *Disenchantment.* It ain't all it was cracked up to be. You've given up your station in life, the world is moving on without you, and your money situation may still be making you nervous. You and your spouse may get on each other's nerves. Some of the outside activities you said you would do aren't working out. Your home may seem too expensive or too difficult to maintain. Your health might become a concern.
4. *Reorientation.* In this stage, you reassess your boredom and financial situation. You may decide to go back to work, consult, or find part-time work. You redo your financial plan and make the proper adjustments. In a sense, you "reretire."
5. *Stability.* You get it together once again, marching to an adjusted lifestyle and financial beat.

What do these "emotional" phases have to do with retirement planning? A lot, actually. Your retirement probably won't go completely as planned, and there will be some lifestyle and financial "redos" along the way. As you "flounder" into retirement, it may cost more, and you may end up making some lifestyle choices you didn't expect. You should try to envision your stability stage and what it will cost in developing your plan.

The Golden Years and Beyond: The Physical and Financial Phases of Retirement

A more useful construct for developing a retirement plan arises from thinking about your physical capabilities and activities in three phases: the "go-go" phase, the "slow-go" phase, and the "no-go" phase.

- *Go-go phase.* In the early Golden Years, you're active, you travel to visit grandkids and others, you check items off the bucket list. You're in good mental and physical health. You try new things. You spend more on travel, education, home upgrades, entertainment, and the like.
- *Slow-go phase.* After perhaps 10 to 20 years, your health, the health of your spouse, or both start to fail, and activity

seems more difficult. More must be budgeted for health care and outside help for routine tasks, while less will be needed for travel, eating out, and so forth.

- *No-go phase.* Now you become dependent on those around you. You rarely go anywhere. Long-term care may be required. A move into a retirement facility is probably needed. A spouse may be lost. An annuity can guarantee income through this phase and can be an important part of a retirement plan. It is possible to buy a deferred annuity early in retirement just to cover this phase.

These phases have obvious financial implications for not only what will be spent but what it will be spent *on.* A good retirement plan breaks down finances for all three phases.

A good retirement plan addresses three phases: the "go-go" phase, the "slow-go" phase, and the "no-go" phase.

Annuities can provide an important income guarantee during the "no-go" phase of retirement.

You can buy a deferred annuity early in retirement just to cover this final phase.

Will You Work?

Working after retirement can obviously bring in extra cash. It doesn't have to be full time or even related to your prior profession. Even retail floor work keeps your mind sharp, keeps you using new digital tools, keeps you engaged with both tasks and people, and it can be fun.

There are downsides. As we'll see in chapter 5, working can complicate your Social Security receipts and how much tax you'll pay on them. For most, working makes sense, but it's a good idea to understand these downsides first.

Will You Own Your Own Home?

I first brought this up in chapter 3, where I reported that 35 percent of the US retirement-age population owns their homes free and clear.

It's important enough that I'll mention it again! Your home can be a liability requiring ongoing rent payment and debt service—or it can be an asset storing value for future retirement income, long-term care expenses, and so forth. Whether you own your home makes a huge difference in your planning and financial security in retirement.

Now the Financial Part

Once you visualize your retirement lifestyle, better done in the three "go" phases introduced above, you can start hanging some numbers on it. When you go to put the numbers into your retirement plan, you'll be basically making a household budget—for 30 years or more. Not a detailed one, mind you; we don't get down to the level of planning grocery or Starbucks money over that time. But we do need to bring in at least an intelligent estimate of what your retirement will cost and then match that with your resources to see what you might still need to add.

How good are people at estimating their expenses? As you can see from table 4.2, people tend to underestimate expenses in retirement, with some 37 percent reporting them higher, while 24 percent report them lower. The good news is that most people report them right on target (35 percent).

TABLE 4.2. How Retiree Experience with Expenses Compares with Expectations (%)

Much higher	16
Somewhat higher	21
About the same	35
Somewhat lower	14
Much lower	10
Don't know	4

Source: Employment Benefit Research Institute, 2015

It's not easy to hang accurate numbers on a lifestyle 20 or 30 years hence; what makes sense is to take your best guess, plan some scenarios, and be willing to change if it gets too difficult to make ends meet. For most people, retirement planning is an iterative process.

Financial Considerations: Spouses, Inflation, Debt, Taxes, Inheritances, Real Estate, and Long-Term Care

Hundreds of variables can influence retirement planning, from housing choices to the number of "snow days" requiring paid-for snow removal and everything in between. Seven factors—spouses, inflation, debt, taxes, inheritances, real estate, and long-term care—play a particularly large role in your planning and number gathering.

Is There a Spouse in the House?

Many of us think of our own individual retirement needs; in fact, most savings plans are set up just that way—as *individual* retirement arrangements. Adding a spouse into the mix changes the planning in several ways:

- Did your spouse work? Is he or she eligible for Social Security? A pension? You will have more income in early stages of retirement drawing from the spouse's Social Security, savings, and other retirement plans.
- Do your resources cover your spouse's life expectancy? Many an individual—particularly the "traditional" husband who brought in the income and made all the financial decisions—has failed to calculate what happens when that spouse is left to fend for him- or herself. Benefits of all kinds will stop or attenuate (as in Social Security changing over into a survivor benefit) when a spouse dies. The spouse may have to live on far less than both did together—a bitter double whammy for the grieving spouse to endure.
- Annuities can be an excellent vehicle to provide for the needs of your spouse once you're gone.

The point is this: A good retirement plan takes a spouse's needs and provisions fully into account, including the changes in entitlements and living costs associated with the change.

Debt: Neither a Borrower Be

Earlier, I alluded to the challenges of *not* owning your own home as you enter retirement. Debt is even worse. If you have large debts, paying them off with your retirement funds can be catastrophic.

You're effectively paying for your preretirement lifestyle with your postretirement savings!

What's more, it's difficult enough to borrow for your retirement as it is. Unless you own your own home or have substantial other assets, you have no way to pay it back, and lenders will look askance at you. If you go into retirement up to your ears in debt, the problem only gets worse; you will have a harder time borrowing for anything.

Here's my best advice: Have a debt-to-zero clause in your retirement plan; try to scratch out those debts before you hit your retirement date.

Inflation: The Silent Killer

Although not such a big consideration as in years past, you still need to keep an eye on inflation. Even at the current (and Fed-targeted) inflation rate of 2 percent, your money can lose a third of its purchasing power in 20 years, as we learned in chapter 1.

Inflation wreaks havoc on fixed investments like bonds. However, its effects can be offset somewhat though stock market gains, which tend to follow inflation in the economy. (Corporate earnings, on which stock prices are largely based, inflate naturally with the economy.) Social Security and some pensions are also indexed against inflation.

Variable annuities are designed to keep up with inflation or even exceed market performance through their market investments, while *fixed indexed annuities* benefit from market gains but are not tied directly to the markets and thus can help keep up with inflation with a lot less risk. I'll discuss both annuity forms in more detail in part 2.

Studies have also shown that retirees consume less as they get older—smaller portion sizes, fewer new pieces of furniture, fewer miles driven. Estimates have retirees consuming about 1 percent less each year.

As a consequence, some retirement planners choose to ignore inflation because it makes the numbers too complicated and because several retirement resources keep up with it anyway. If you're a very conservative investor unlikely to take the risks necessary to keep up with economic growth, inflation planning becomes more important.

Don't Forget the Tax Man

You experienced the tax bite all through your working years. Guess what? It doesn't stop at retirement, but it does slow down somewhat—that's the good news.

Your tax rate is likely to be lower in retirement. First of all, you no longer pay employment taxes (FICA). Second, your Social Security is taxed at a reduced rate or not at all (see chapter 5). Third, you probably earn less money than you did in your working years. Your tax rates are likely lower—although if you pay off your home like I've been advocating, you also lose the interest deduction.

Your tax rate may drop from the 30–40 percent range (state taxes included) to the 15–20 percent range, something much more affordable. Elaborate tax calculators take taxes into account, but taxes are hard to predict and many choose to do their retirement planning on a pretax basis just to keep the numbers simple and comparable to their gross income figures when they were working.

And That's Not All: Other Special Considerations

As you put together your retirement plan, the following additional considerations may apply.

Lucky You: There's an Inheritance

Of course, if you have a large and certain inheritance on the way, it should be figured into the retirement plan. The only problem is, you can't be sure when it will arrive! For most, it's an extra security factor—or a source of extra cruise vacation money—when it comes. Unless, of course, the death of an elder is imminent. You might also consider redeploying inherited wealth into lifetime protection for you and yours through an annuity.

Are You Landed Gentry?

I've commented on the virtues of owning your own home, debt free. But if you have rental real estate, especially if it's paid for, it can provide a good steady (and often rising) form of income, especially in your early "go-go" retirement years.

However, you should be concerned about what happens as you get older and are less able or willing to perform your duties as a landlord. At some point in your planning, you may want to consider selling the real estate—removing the landlord burden—and buying guaranteed-income annuities with the proceeds.

When You Really Become "No-Go": Long-Term Care

Lurking as a possibility for all of us is the scary idea that, yes, someday we may become chronically ill or incapacitated and be unable to perform the normal activities of daily living (ADL) like feeding ourselves, putting clothes on, and so forth. We may need some form of long-term care in a nursing home or some such.

According to AARP, some 68 percent of us 65 or older will be cognitively impaired or need help with at least two ADLs during our lives. Our living expenses will soar from a couple thousand a month to $5,000 or $7,000 or more—figure $85,000 a year with inflation; figure an average stay of two to three years.

You can fund these special-care needs by buying long-term care (LTC) insurance, but it's expensive, especially if you do what most do and wait until you're older to buy it. You may not qualify due to health.

Some also anticipate using equity from a sold primary residence to cover LTC—that's a good plan, if you stick to it. And some may add a rider covering LTC to an annuity already providing guaranteed income for life.

> Annuities can be tailor-made to take care of the needs of a spouse upon death.
>
> Inheritances or other lump-sum asset sales during retirement can be converted into annuities to provide guaranteed income.
>
> Long-term care needs can also be handled with special annuity riders.

What's in a Good Retirement Plan?

There's no given or standard format for a retirement plan. No two are alike, just as no two individuals or couples are alike.

A good retirement plan is whatever it takes to get you to think methodically about what you need, what you have, and where the gaps and weak spots lie in your current and future situation. Nothing more, nothing less.

I don't care about the format so much, but I do believe that a reasonable, actionable retirement plan includes the following 12 steps:

1. *Create a lifestyle vision.* Who will you be, what will you do, where will you live, how will you live (will you own a boat?), and so forth.
2. *Estimate life expectancy for you and your spouse.* Once you've done this, add 5 or 10 years just in case.
3. *Estimate monthly income needs.* The best plans do it phase by phase: the "go-go," "slow-go," and "no-go" phases, and after departure of spouse. This can be based on a percentage of current income.
4. *Add a cushion for contingencies.* Try to have a year to two years' savings or more for who knows what.
5. *Decide on retirement age for you and your spouse.* What retirement age works best for both of you, considering your careers, your retirement aspirations, your health, your finances, where you live and want to live, and so forth.
6. *Estimate entitlements and pensions.* Figure out what to expect from Social Security for you and for your spouse (see chapter 5).
7. *Estimate irregular windfalls and expenses.* There may be inheritances, home sales, new car purchases, and so on.
8. *Calculate the "gap."* The "gap" is the savings needed to meet what entitlements and pensions don't cover. We'll look at some calculators to help with this in chapter 11.
9. *Repeat steps 1–8 to adjust for gaps.* Use a later retirement age, for example.
10. *Decide how much "guaranteed income" you need for life.* If this is greater than your Social Security and pension check(s), consider an annuity.

11. *Review with a financial advisor.* It helps to have another trained, experienced, and unbiased set of eyes review your work. It's worth a couple of hundred bucks.
12. *"Publish" the plan.* This sounds simple, but most don't (see table 4.3). Publishing the plan formalizes the effort, which usually makes it a stronger effort; it also gives you something to look back on and adjust if necessary.

Okay, So How Much Planning Does Everyone Else Do?

Once again, we're back in "Keep up with the Joneses" land by showing, according to the EBRI survey, just how many people have actually done some of the key steps outlined above.

TABLE 4.3. Planning Steps Taken by Workers to Prepare for Retirement (%)

Thought about how time would be occupied in retirement	63
Estimated how much monthly income needed	45
Estimated SSA benefit at retirement age	40
Talked with a financial advisor about retirement planning	35
Calculated how much money spouse would need to cover health expenses in retirement	25
Prepared a formal, written plan for retirement	16
Calculated how much money needed for retirement	48

Source: Employment Benefit Research Institute, 2015

I was surprised to see that "writing it down" is actually the least often performed step! Do people really expect to carry a rock-solid, actionable retirement plan around in their heads? Heck, I can't even remember an amount on a check I wrote this morning!

The better news in my opinion is that 48 percent surveyed had actually calculated how much they needed for retirement.

Putting Together a Plan and Getting the Right Help

So you finally decide to put together a retirement plan. Now what?

You can start with the list outlined in "What's in a Good Retirement Plan?" Some of these steps, like creating a lifestyle vision, involve a conversation at the kitchen table, over a glass of wine, or perhaps on a special minivacation designed for the purpose. From there, most of the steps involve collecting some data, making some calculations, and making some adjustments based on those calculations.

Finally, as I advocated previously, a plan isn't really a plan until you agree on it and write it down. Do this.

Along the way, you may or may not seek the help of an advisor. I recommend at least checking your work with one; paying the $150 fee or so to get a second look and a second opinion is helpful. You may want to involve an advisor for more steps along the way, including the visualizing at the beginning of the process.

If you do choose a professional advisor, know that some are better than others for this purpose. Many so-called advisors are really financial salespeople, compensated by commissions generated from the financial "products" (mutual funds, etc.) that they sell. Here are two important recommendations:

- *Find a "fee-only" certified financial planner (CFP).* CFPs have the broadest knowledge of the financial considerations of a retirement plan. They are not just limited to giving investment advice; they'll help you through both financial and nonfinancial considerations. Most CFPs are or are linked closely to Registered Investment Advisors (RIAs), so they can legally give investment advice. Fewer know about annuities because they are insurance products marketed by licensed insurance agents, but a good CFP should be able to include annuities in their advice. "Fee-only" (not "fee-based") advisors are paid by the hour or by a percentage of assets under management—not for selling you something. The Financial Planning Association website (fpanet.org) is a good way to locate a fee-only advisor.
- *Work with a fiduciary.* If you're working with a CFP or an RIA, chances are you're already working with someone sworn

and duty-bound to put your interests ahead of theirs. Be careful about retail stockbrokers and other "advisors" not carrying the "letters" noted above—some are fiduciaries, some are not. When working with insurance agents and others promoting annuities, know that many are not held to the fiduciary standard, although that may be changing because new initiatives from the Department of Labor may hold annuity and other insurance advisors working with retirement savings to a fiduciary standard. Requiring a fiduciary standard should be a no-brainer for anyone selling a financial product, but it is surprising how few advisors in some circles have made this commitment.

- *For annuities, work with a licensed independent insurance agent.* When it's time to learn more about how annuities fit into your retirement income plan, find a knowledgeable state-licensed insurance agent with a strong annuity background. Independent agents (not single-company agents) are preferred because they can offer annuities from many carriers, giving you more choices among the hundreds of annuity products available. The payouts generated by these products and their riders can vary substantially, by as much as 30 percent in some cases.

Where Do We Go from Here?

The remaining chapters in part 1 examine the major pillars of your retirement plan.

- Chapter 5 gives some fast facts on Social Security entitlements and how secure they really are.
- Chapter 6 explores the nature of volatility and risk in current markets and how they make any retirement nest egg less than secure.
- Chapter 7 shows how the timing of market swings can also make your savings less than secure.
- Chapter 8 explores retirement planning tools and calculators—tools to help you with the math of retirement, including the "4 percent rule" and a simple 15-minute approach to determining how much savings you actually need.

- Part 2 (chapters 9–14) shifts the conversation to how to deploy savings to accomplish the specific goal of providing guaranteed lifetime income beyond Social Security (and a pension if you are lucky enough to have one). Such rock-solid safety and income security is accomplished through the use of annuities—I'll describe what annuities are and how to use them effectively.

By the Numbers

- **68.** The percentage of workers who are "very" or "somewhat" confident in their financial preparation for retirement (But 64 percent also say they are "behind" in their retirement preparation.)
- **37.** The percentage of workers who say that expenses in retirement are "somewhat" or "much" higher than expected (About 35 percent say it is what they expect.)
- **24.** The percentage of workers who say that retirement expenses are lower than they expected
- **63.** The percentage of workers who have visualized their retirement
- **48.** The percentage of workers who have calculated what they need to retire (But only 16 percent have written their retirement plans into formal documents.)
- **68.** The percentage of individuals over 65 who will need help with cognitive impairment or at least two activities of daily living in retirement
- **$85,000.** The average annual cost of a nursing home

CHAPTER 5

SOCIAL SECURITY

Rock Solid and Forever?

"S*avings? No, I don't have any stinkin' savings. I'm just going to retire and live on my Social Security.*"

I'm sure you know someone who has said this or have heard someone say this. Indeed, Social Security was conceived to help retirees in the Depression who once depended on their now-strapped families for support. But with an average annual payout of $15,936 (2015), it was never designed to pay the full retirement bill.

Yet, as the statistics from earlier chapters show, a sizeable number of people cling to this myth. Not only is it not true (as we learned in chapter 1, Social Security only covers about 39 percent of an average retirement), but I also find that it gives many retirees a false sense of security.

Worse, while retiree benefits are still considered the hazardous "third rail" of American politics, something has to give eventually. The government trust fund that pays out Social Security is destined to go to zero by the year 2035 if nothing is changed, indicating that something probably *will* change by then. That change could well be for the worse so far as retiree benefits are concerned.

Here's the bottom line: Social Security isn't enough, and it may not last forever in its present form.

In this chapter, I give a short description of how Social Security works, what you can expect of it, and how to build it into your retirement plan. More detail is available in several books and websites (Laurence Kotlikoff's *Get What's Yours* is one good book, and the Social Security Administration [SSA] website [https://www.ssa.gov] is pretty good, too). This chapter covers what *most* need to know to plan their Social Security in retirement.

The Best of the Best: If Only It Were Enough

Social Security is pure magic. It's the best annuity you'll ever own—and it's free! Like an annuity, it guarantees income for life. But it goes beyond. Payment is guaranteed by the government. It has built-in inflation protection (which you can buy with an annuity). It has spouse and survivor protection (which you can also buy with an annuity). It is tax-preferenced. It comes with no market risk and no annual fees or costs. What could be better?

Once more time: Social Security is the best retirement plan—the best annuity—you can own. And you don't even have to "buy" Social Security; there are no outlays (save for the mandatory FICA taxes you've paid all your life) and no sales commissions.

It's yours—automatically and for free. The problem is, to repeat, that it covers less than half of a typical retirement, and it may change well within the planning horizon for most retirees.

Just the Basics

In addition to the traditional and obvious retirement benefits, Social Security offers an array of other benefits covering special situations: spousal benefits, survivor benefits, divorcee spousal benefits, disability benefits, certain child benefits. I'll touch on spousal, survivor, and divorcee benefits because they may touch your retirement planning calculations.

Joining the Social Security Club

It's pretty simple: To be eligible for Social Security, just be a US citizen (or be in the country legally) and work, either as an employee or as a self-employment-tax-paying individual, for 40 quarters—that is, 10 years. Or be married for 40 quarters (10 years) to collect a spousal benefit.

A Gold Watch from the Government: When Can You Collect Social Security?

When you (and your spouse) actually file to collect Social Security can make a big difference. Generally, the longer you wait, the more you'll get, and much of the calculation hinges on what the SSA calls "full retirement age" (FRA).

Collecting in Full: The "Full Retirement Age"

The US government has set the following ages—depending on when you were born—as the "full retirement age" for Social Security:

- 1937 and before: 65
- 1943–54: 66
- 1960 and after: 67

Between 1938 and 1943 and between 1955 and 1959, the FRA advances two months for every year; thus, the FRA for someone born in 1956 is 66 years, four months.

Early and Late Retirement

Early retirement can be taken as early as age 62. In theory, you don't lose anything by retiring early. The SSA calculates a full actuarial amount you would normally receive through your life expectancy and then prorates it across the number of years you collect. If you retire at 62 instead of, say, 66, your payment gets four extra years in the denominator for the monthly payment calculation. The resulting difference is called an *early retirement deduction.*

"Late" retirement can happen up until age 70. If you retire at age 70, you receive *delayed retirement credits,* which effectively is the result of reducing the aforementioned denominator.

Currently, delaying retirement from age 62 increases your monthly payment about 8 percent for each year delayed. This compounds, so delaying from age 62 to age 70 results in a payment some 76 percent larger than you would receive at age 62—but of course, over a period of time that is eight years shorter.

Incidentally, a vast plurality of retirees claim Social Security at 62:

- In 2012, 38 percent of all claims for men occurred at age 62, 43 percent for women.
- The next highest claiming age was 66—18 percent for men, 12 percent for women.
- Next was age 65, with 12 percent for both genders.
- Only 1 percent of men and 2 percent of women waited until age 70.

> From age 62 to age 70, every year you delay retirement results in an 8 percent increase in monthly benefits.
>
> If you delay from age 62 to age 70, your monthly benefit will be 76 percent higher.

Okay, So How Much Do You Get?

Now that we know when you get it, the next question is, How much do you get? What is your expected monthly income at FRA?

Like most things with Social Security, the calculation is a little beyond our scope. But not surprisingly, it's tied to how much you earned during your working years.

And it is very progressive, meaning that Congress wanted to give some preference to low-income workers, who need a retirement safety net just as much or more than higher-income earners.

So Congress based the Social Security formula on something called a primary insurance amount (PIA). The PIA formula sums up your average earnings over your best 35 years of employment (or self-employment) to arrive at something referred to as an average indexed monthly earnings (AIME). The formula calculates three tiers to arrive at your PIA—your estimated payment at FRA:

- 90 percent of your first $826 in AIME
- 32 percent of earnings between $826 and $4,980
- 15 percent of the amount above $4,980

An example of this calculation can be found at the SSA website: https://www.ssa.gov/OACT/ProgData/retirebenefit2.html.

You Don't Have to Calculate Your Own Social Security

Social Security formulas are very complex, and they're based on data you would not have readily available, like the AIME described above.

You can get a handy personalized one-page summary of your probable Social Security benefits at any time (assuming you qualify for Social Security) by setting up an account online with the SSA at https://www.ssa.gov/myaccount.

It only takes a few minutes and gives you not only a glimpse into your retirement benefit but also a look at survivor benefits, disability benefits, and other figures helpful for planning.

These online calculations are intended to be estimates only; for more complex situations involving spousal retirement what-ifs, divorce situations, and so on, it is advisable to contact someone at a local SSA office or to try one of the paid-for services, an example of which is described at the end of this chapter.

Built-in Inflation Protection: The Cost-of-Living Adjustment

Based on a variation of the consumer price index (CPI), Social Security benefits are inflated almost every year. Here is one change to keep tabs on: Proposals have been made to switch the cost-of-living-allowance basis to a tamer version of the CPI or to another index. This is the sort of thing you must watch out for with Social Security—and why having annuities to back up guaranteed lifetime income isn't a bad idea.

Can You Still Work and Collect Social Security?

You want to collect Social Security, but you also want to continue part time as a consulting professional, as a book author, as a Wal-Mart greeter, or whatever. What happens? What are the rules?

The rules say you can work. However, you'll be subject to what's known as the retirement earnings test, and some of your Social Security can be held back if you fail. Clearly the designers of the test were trying to prevent you from working and retiring early to collect Social Security benefits.

If you earn more than $15,720 in addition to your Social Security between the ages of 62 and 65, the SSA reclaims $1 in Social Security for every $2 you earn. This amount is not lost, however—it simply goes back into your Social Security account and is paid out later when you do reach FRA.

For ages 65 to FRA, there is a similar limit, but it rises to $41,880 and you lose $1 for every $3 in earnings. There is no earnings test beyond your FRA.

> Between ages 62 and 65, there is no penalty for working and collecting Social Security if you earn less than $15,720.
>
> Between 65 and FRA, that threshold is $41,880.
>
> Beyond that, you can earn as much as you want.

Taxation of Social Security Benefits

Very little in life is free of taxes, and Social Security benefits are no exception. While the benefits are taxed, they are taxed at a far reduced rate, and the earnings themselves are not considered in the calculation—only income outside of Social Security. This means that if you have substantial other income, like dividends and interest income, you *might* have to pay *some* taxes on your Social Security.

Some consider it unfair to have to pay taxes on Social Security—you already paid taxes on the dollars going into the system through your FICA or self-employment taxes. Others marvel at the reduced taxes as another "one-off" feature of Social Security unattainable with other forms of retirement income.

Here's the simple truth about Social Security taxation:

- For singles with incomes under $25,000 (not including the Social Security) and married couples filing jointly earning under $32,000, Social Security benefits are tax-free.
- For singles with income between $25,000 and $34,000 and married-filing-jointly couples earning between $32,000

and $44,000, up to half of Social Security benefits are taxable at the marginal tax rate.

- For singles above $34,000 and married couples earning more than $44,000, 85 percent of Social Security benefits are taxable.

These tax rules really mean that a married couple collecting $25,000 in annual Social Security could earn a total of $58,000 ($34,000 outside income plus $25,000 in Social Security) before any of it becomes taxable. It's a healthy tax break.

Maximizing What *You* Get from Social Security

Social Security is designed to provide a basic retirement stipend to an individual. But it's also set up to cover spouses, survivors (if a spouse dies), divorcees, surviving children under 19, and disability, among other "special cases." Old age is but one thing Social Security protects against.

How much you get from Social Security depends on how much you earn during your working years and when you claim it. Thus the answer to "How do I get the most Social Security?" is simply, wait. Wait as long as you can. Wait past 62 to FRA and you'll get 25 percent more. Wait until age 70 and you'll get 76 percent more.

End of discussion? Not quite.

Married, Widowed, Divorced? Timing Can Be Everything

Things start to get complicated when you have a spouse or if you're a widow/widower or a divorcee. Here are some sample rules, pointers, and strategies for maximizing Social Security for married couples and other situations:

- If you've been married for one year (there are a few exceptions), a spouse is eligible for either his or her own earned Social Security or up to half of yours, whichever is larger.
- A spouse must wait for you to file to collect his or her benefit.
- A spouse claiming a spousal benefit at full retirement age is eligible for half your benefit. If the spouse files for early retirement, that benefit is reduced up to 30 percent if he or she files at age 62.

- The question becomes how long to wait before you file. The answer depends on your relative ages and need for income:
    - If you and your spouse are about the same age, you maximize if you both file at full retirement age. If you wait until age 70, you forgo several years of spousal benefits.
    - If the older partner (and main breadwinner) is slightly older, he or she should file when the partner reaches full retirement age (the older partner will earn delayed retirement credits for the few extra years waited).
    - If the older partner is more than four years older, it makes sense to wait until age 70 to file and for the trailing spouse to wait until FRA. That maximizes both retirement and survivor benefits (a survivor gets an amount equal to the decedent's benefit, which should be taken if it exceeds the retiree's benefit).
    - If you were born before 1953, you can actually claim a spousal benefit before reaching FRA, then build up more credit and file for your own benefit when you hit FRA. You can't do this if you were born after 1954.
- Divorcees are eligible for the full spousal benefit at full retirement age if the marriage lasted 10 years or more. A spouse with his or her own benefits exceeding this spousal benefit should, of course, file for their own Social Security. Early retirement costs up to 30 percent if retired at 62.
- Survivors are eligible for 100 percent of the decedent's payment after being married for nine months.
- Waiting to FRA (or even age 70) enhances not only individual but also survivor benefits.

This list was designed to introduce you to some of the possibilities—and to scare you out of doing your own Social Security plan! If I've scared you off, I've done my job! It is by no means complete. I strongly suggest getting help from the SSA and/or doing some of your own modeling based on the tool described in the sidebar "A Worthwhile $40 Investment."

A Worthwhile $40 Investment

To say the least, the rules and mathematics of Social Security are daunting. Why, the SSA's own personnel often get it wrong when making complex Social Security calculations. How can you maximize a situation where you're five years older than your spouse, he or she has a fair income and a disabled kid and, God forbid, you're terminally ill and he or she might be eligible for a survivor benefit in a few years?

Such calculations aren't for the faint of heart, nor really for the ambitious do-it-yourselfer. I mentioned Boston University Economics professor Laurence Kotlikoff and his book *Get What's Yours* earlier, but even this book won't do the math for you.

Instead, I recommend spending $40 on a license to a planning tool called "Maximize My Social Security" at https://www.maximizemysocialsecurity.com.

For 40 bucks, you'll get not only estimates of what's coming your way but also strategies to maximize your total Social Security income.

Not a bad deal. It could turn out to be the best 40 bucks you ever spent.

Here's the bottom line: Any retirement plan should include a realistic and maximized appraisal of estimated Social Security payments over time. The SSA personal summary gives you a pretty good idea where you stand as an individual; things get tricky (and scary) as your family situation gets more complex.

Get help.

What Could Possibly Go Wrong with Social Security?

Social Security is perceived to be the safest and, well, most secure of all retirement resources. After all, it is backed by the full faith and credit of the US government. What could possibly go wrong? What do you need to beware of?

- *Trust fund depletion.* Social Security is spending more than it is taking in, and by law it must be self-sufficient. Yet in 1950 there were 16.5 workers for every beneficiary, by 2000 there were 3.4, and by 2035 there will be only 2.8 workers per beneficiary. The trust fund will be depleted by 2035 but would break even with a 25 percent reduction in benefits. The probable outcome of this gap is a raise in collections by raising the ceiling on wage income (or capital gains income) taxed. But if the political winds blow the wrong way, could retirement ages, benefit levels, spousal benefits, and so on be tinkered with? I think it's a possibility you should watch out for.

- *Privatization.* Various proposals over the years have called for the privatization of Social Security—really, the ability to invest the funds now committed to the Social Security Trust Fund (privately, that is) by investment advisors in stocks, bonds, and so on. Of course, this may bring higher returns and more "solvency," but it also brings market risk. Since we all count on Social Security as our one bastion of retirement income for life (unless we own an annuity), it could put us all at more risk. If it does happen someday, it may increase your need for guaranteed lifetime income.

Given current benefits, age ranges, and rules, the Social Security trust fund will be depleted by 2035.

A 25 percent reduction in benefits would eliminate the deficit. But there are other ways.

Is Social Security a Ponzi Scheme?

Many critics have called Social Security a Ponzi scheme superseding even the most evil intentions of Bernard Madoff and Mr. Ponzi himself.

The main idea, of course, is that current retirees don't receive their own contributions; they receive the contributions of current workers. Sort of like new investors' funds being used to pay off early investors.

This is a bad idea—especially when the music stops and there are no more current workers or investors.

The last workers in the party will never collect, just like Madoff's later investors ended up with nothing because their investments had been used to pay off early investors.

Is this fear legit? In a word, no:

- Social Security is backed by the full faith and credit of the federal government. They have the power to legislate change; the system will not just "run out."
- A typical Ponzi scheme is characterized by reliance on an ever-growing number of contributors. If anything, Social Security has the opposite.
- A Ponzi scheme is opaque; nobody knows what's really going on with the money inside of it. Social Security, on the other hand, is very transparent, with regular, open, and detailed reporting on sources and uses of funds. There is no deception.
- The intent of Social Security is to protect its constituents, not to take advantage of them. Big difference.

So while Social Security has its faults and may be subject to change or market risk, there is nothing deceptive about it.

Bottom Line: Safe for Now but Not Enough

The bottom line, as I've shown, is that Social Security is the best retirement resource you can have, and everybody has it if they have logged 40 quarters of work. The main problem with Social Security is that at 39 percent of average retirement income needs, it just doesn't provide enough for most retirees to maintain their accustomed standard of living.

As such, Social Security income must be supplemented with something to guarantee retirement security and sought-after living standards. Pensions, of course, help, but even if available, leave an income gap for most.

The real challenge is filling the gap with safe, reliable, and guaranteed income sources. Most people fill the gap with retirement savings. But as I'll show in the next two chapters, those savings, particularly if invested for decent returns in the markets, are subject to the forces of risk and volatility, over which you have no control.

This is why I advocate annuities to fill the income gap—at least part of it, anyway. Annuities take up where Social Security (and pensions) leave off, providing guaranteed income for life, much as Social Security does.

With annuities, a far more substantial portion of your retirement needs can be covered for good.

> Annuities can extend the best virtue of Social Security—guaranteed income for life—to cover a greater portion of retirement needs.
>
> They also serve as insurance against changes and reductions in benefits.

By the Numbers

- **39.** The average percentage of retirement needs covered by Social Security
- **$15,936.** The average annual Social Security individual payment (2015)
- **8.** The percentage a monthly benefit rises for every year waited after age 62 to retire
- **76.** A monthly benefit for an age-70 retiree is 76 percent higher than for an age-62 retiree
- **38, 43.** The percentage of all Social Security claims filed at age 62 for men and women, respectively
- **1, 2.** The percentage of all Social Security claims filed at age 70 for men and women, respectively
- **$25,000, $32,000.** The amount of income *besides Social Security* you can earn—single and married, respectively—and keep your Social Security tax-free

CHAPTER 6

SAVINGS AND SAFETY, PART 1

Market Risk and Volatility

Especially these days, when you think about retirement savings, you think about investments. Gone are the days where you could just stuff cash into your passbook savings account (anyone remember those?) and have it earn a guaranteed 5 percent with virtually no risk. Hindsight might be 20/20, but 5 percent sounds pretty darned good nowadays, right?

Just as pensions have vaporized over the years, such fixed and virtually guaranteed high investment returns have gone the way of the dodo bird. Now, since Social Security and pensions typically fall well short of covering all of your retirement savings, you need to have savings for retirement, and you will want to invest those savings. For maximum retirement security, you'll want to invest those savings to grow—or at least to keep up with inflation.

Now, here's the problem: You can invest "safely" in bonds or other fixed income investments, but you'll earn returns scarcely better than inflation—unless you buy riskier bonds. Or you can invest in stocks, which participate in the growth of the economy and thus earn twice what bonds do over the long run. But don't forget—they participate in economic bad times, too.

In a nutshell, the enticing returns of stocks also bring with them volatility and risk. As we'll see in this chapter, investing is good. You should invest at least some portion of that nest egg.

You sense a "but" coming—and here it is: you need to be aware of the volatility and risk you take on when you make these investments. Don't get me wrong—investing works out for most people most of the time. But it can go badly as well, because of the risks, volatility, and timing of that volatility.

In this chapter, I discuss volatility and risk and how they can affect your nest egg. Chapter 7 then shows how the ravages of bad timing—bad markets in the first few years of retirement—can affect that nest egg as well.

Here's the upshot: Investing is good, and you should invest. But there's good reason not to put all of your (nest) eggs in one investing basket. Once again, fixed and fixed indexed annuities, with their income guarantee and insulation from volatility and market risk, can be the peace-of-mind alternative to the rocky, risky world of investing.

It's a Winner, But . . .

Over the years, the stock market has been a winning bet. According to the St. Louis Federal Reserve, the markets, as measured by the S&P 500 on a total return basis—including dividends—have earned 11.41 percent, including dividends and distributions per year from 1928 through 2015.

Now that sounds pretty darned enriching, and it is. Eleven percent? Put that figure into any compounding model and a few thousand saved here and there become millions in a normal working life.

Okay, that would be great, and we could put this retirement planning book down right now and head to the beach. Right?

Wrong. The 11.41 percent includes inflation of roughly 4 to 5 percent and dividends of about 2 to 3 percent, leaving real economic growth of about 3 to 5 percent. So, you say, GDP hasn't consistently grown this much? You're right; it hasn't. But S&P 500–sized companies also grow by taking market share from smaller local companies (e.g., Wal-Mart vs. small-town stores), so the markets can, and do, grow faster than GDP.

So—especially in light of growing dividends for stocks (contrasting with fixed interest yields for bonds)—shouldn't we be putting ever greater portions of our nest eggs in stocks?

The problems—there are two of them—are volatility and its close first cousin, risk. Because of volatility and risk, markets don't always return 11.41 percent. They just average 11.41 percent, and that figure is no longer so solid. (As we learned in chapter 2, the average annual gain has been only 3.5 percent since 2000.) Volatility and risk: I'll define and expand on these two gremlins right now.

Volatility: On the Rise

First, let's get a couple of definitions out of the way:

- Volatility is the largely directionless up and down movement of, say, a stock price or index. Volatility can drive the price upward or downward—either way making you lose sleep due to the change itself and the fact that a downward "spike" might not be simple volatility but a signal of a larger, more painful downturn.
- Risk is the possibility of something going fundamentally wrong with your investment ("internal" risk) or with the larger economic environment ("external" risk) or something bad happening to your investments because of your own mistakes, lack of time, or bad habits ("personal" risk). When you invest, you take on all three risks. Volatility can drive an investment up or down; risk can only drive it downward.

Now, for a variety of reasons, volatility is on the rise. Let me explain by example, then come back to those reasons.

When you invest your precious capital in a business (by buying stocks) or in a basket of businesses (by buying a fund), you're subjecting yourself to the ups and downs of the market and of the business(es) you're investing in. There can be no better way to illustrate than to show the following chart of 86 years of stock market performance (see figure 6.1).

The chart in figure 6.1 looks rather like a profile of the US Great Plains and their transition to the Rocky Mountains, doesn't it? *Done well over the past few years. Up and to the right. That's a good thing; most of us have made money.*

But look at the ups and downs! In recent years, the change—both in magnitude and in percent—from one year, one month, one day,

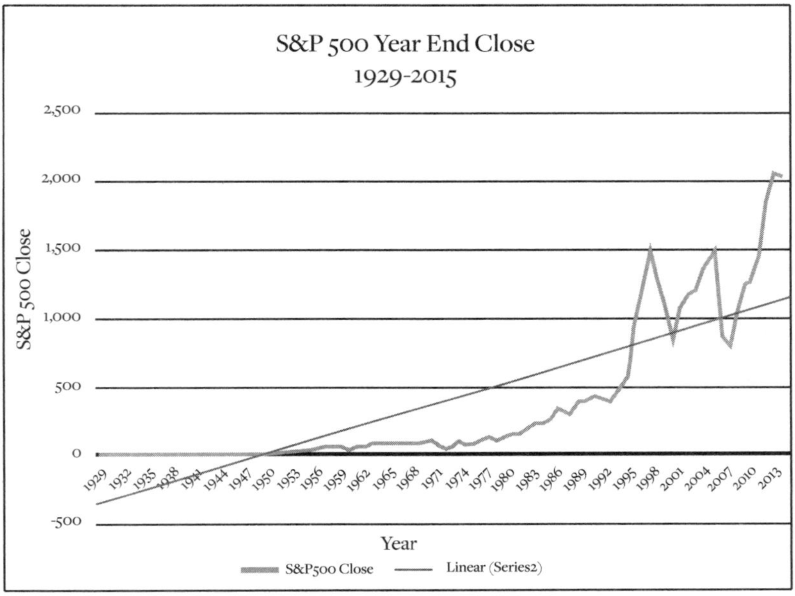

Figure 6.1. S&P 500 Year-End Close, 1929–2015

and even five minutes has expanded big time. Slow, steady gains are hardly the norm anymore. I'll explore some of the reasons why later in this chapter.

Yes, Stocks Really Have Done Well

So how much better have stocks performed? Are they worth the risk? Worth the trouble?

The answer is pretty much "yes"—for part of your portfolio, at least.

According to data compiled by the St. Louis Federal Reserve, stock market performance, as measured by the S&P 500 Index, has pretty much doubled that of bonds.

Inclusive of yields, from 1928 through 2015, stocks have averaged a gain of 11.41 percent a year, including dividends, inflation, and real growth.

Bonds, on the other hand, have gained 5.23 percent per year total as measured by the 10-year US Treasury bond.

More recently, those gains have been attenuated as volatility and the Great Recession have taken their toll. Over the 10-year period of 2006–15, stocks have gained 7.25 percent compared to 4.71 percent for bonds.

So What's the Problem with Stocks?

Invest it, gain 11.41 percent a year, and walk away. No worries, right? Those healthy returns, and why would you need to protect anything with an annuity or some other "guaranteed" income vehicle?

The problem—as you probably guessed—is that these return "ducks" don't always walk in a row. In fact, the number of years where the S&P 500 Index return was anywhere close to 11.41 percent is pretty small.

Consider figure 6.2. While the distribution of "up" and "down" years is (1) fairly "normal" and (2) happily skewed toward years "up" more than the 11.41 percent mean, the chart clearly shows that you can't count on 11.41 percent, or anything close, in a given year.

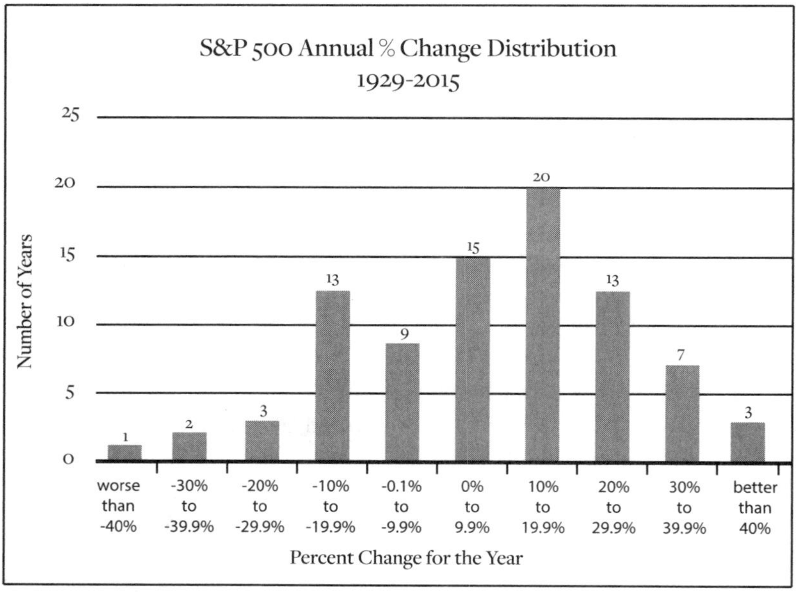

Figure 6.2. S&P 500 Annual Percent Change Distribution

So when investing in stocks, you must embrace this volatility and the likelihood that things will come out (far) better than average, or perhaps (far) worse. You're pretty likely to come out ahead in the long run (those who have researched it have found the average nest egg to last or even grow in 97 percent of the 30-year periods since the 1920s), but you don't know. You can't be too sure—about anything.

Such uncertainty has caused lost sleep and anxiety for many a retiree. This wall of worry, combined with the work and attention good investing requires, argues well for putting at least some of your nest egg in solid, guaranteed income annuities.

You can throw this "up and down" stuff over the wall to someone else. Guaranteed lifetime income becomes their problem, not yours. And sure, like any insurance coverage, you pay something for this privilege. But peace of mind—especially when you're in your "slow go" or "no go" years—can be, as the commercials say, "priceless."

> Stocks have performed very well over the years—more than twice as well as bonds. But this performance is hardly consistent from year to year.
>
> Peace of mind against this wall of worry—especially in retirement years—can be "priceless."
>
> Annuities can provide this peace of mind.

Taking Apart Risk and Volatility

Earlier in the chapter, I promised some detail on the causes of risk and volatility. The idea is to make you more sensitive to the wide assortment of factors that can make things unstable and/or go wrong. Again, these factors don't necessarily make investing in stocks and the US economy a bad idea. They should instead give you a better sense of how many of your hard-earned chips to put on this table and how risky a hand you might want to play once you decide.

Why Volatility?

In the strictest sense, volatility is up and down movement without a particular direction. As such, and because your retirement investments are by nature a long-term venture, volatility should be something you can ignore.

But we all know that when the markets get into one of those moods where the Dow is down 300 one day, up 100 the next, up 250 the third day, and down 150 the next, you have every right to be nervous. Obviously the demons of uncertainty are hard at work. And just when will the ups and downs cease to include the ups?

It's About Change, and It's About the Unknown

The truth is simple: Changes in how business works—many of those changes brought on by the digital age—have led quite naturally to an increase in volatility. Things change bigger, and they change faster. And because volatility is driven by both reality and perception, perceptions change bigger and faster than ever before.

In a nutshell, volatility is about unknowns. How will the economy fare next year? How will a change in interest rates, a China slowdown, or an act of war affect a business or the economy in general? If the future were to be known, there would be a lot less volatility.

But of course, the future is an unknown. As they say regarding change, the only thing that is constant is change itself. The change is a given, but certain aspects of the modern digital era make the change happen faster and make it hit harder. Specific sources of volatility include, but are not limited to

- Business volatility. If you had invested in the hottest investment of the day in the 1880s—railroads—for the most part, you would have invested in a business whose cycle lasted 100-plus years. If you had invested in radio in the 1920s, maybe the advent of television shortened the cycle. Today's businesses—computers, the Internet, biotech—have much shorter cycles. Microsoft has enjoyed a 25-year heyday, but its core technologies are being replaced by the cloud, Google Chrome and Android, and others. They are now doing a pretty good job of playing catchup, but the point is simply that most businesses change faster and may disappear altogether unless they reinvent themselves several times over the years. Technology and the rapid pace of change in consumer tastes—again a product of the digital age—work together to drive this.

- News in a flash. Whatever happens—or doesn't happen, for that matter—circles the globe at the speed of light. To repeat, volatility is driven by both perceptions and reality. When both perceptions and reality can be altered in an instant, the potential to increase and amplify volatility is obvious. "Bandwagons" of followers are created faster, become bigger, and change directions more rapidly with every bit of new news.
- Globalization. The 'round-the-world nature of business leads to more volatility—a shortage of a key input, for instance, will be felt across a wider area. Supply chain problems, changes of tastes, and so forth—again, real and perceived—become worldwide phenomena, thus increasing volatility.
- Rapid-fire trading. Fueled by rapid change and rapid information and enabled by the power of sophisticated real-time trading systems, owners of securities can acquire or dump securities in fractions of seconds. Once again, big changes can come to securities prices as everyone jumps on the bandwagon at the same instant.
- Financial policy. The Federal Reserve has always had the power to influence the economy and markets, but in recent years, it has become more "liberal" in using it. The Fed seems to want to play a greater role in managing the ups and downs of the markets, unemployment, and at the end of the day, inflation. Interest rate hikes—real and potential—have more profound effects on the markets than they once did.

Volatility is up-and-down movement, usually directionless, around an average or trend.

It is caused my many factors, mainly unknowns and perceptions of those unknowns.

It is magnified by the speed of business, the speed of communication, and the speed of the markets.

Flying Way Out of Formation: Black Swans

Every now and then, an event will occur way out of the range of what anyone would call "normal." It's not hard to think of such events: September 11, Pearl Harbor, the Deepwater Horizon Gulf of Mexico oil spill of 2010, the Fukushima earthquake in Japan in 2011. It goes without saying—these events disrupt certain investments for sure (like oil giant BP for Deepwater Horizon) and/or markets in general (like the rest).

Just as a black swan is highly unusual around a group of white swans, black swan events, as described by author Nassem Nicholas Taleb in his 2010 book The Black Swan, are events beyond the realm of the normal patterns of history, science, finance, industry or technology. The problem is, they are rare enough that most people are blind to their possibility and fail to see their possibility until after the fact. They rationalize, "I should have seen that" and often dump their investments at a loss in the wake of the event.

As black swans usually transcend the limits of "rational" expectations, the response is typically emotional. Even if your response isn't emotional, they can take a lot of value out of your retirement investment accounts.

The key to dealing with black swans is to strengthen your fortress against them—really, to avoid them altogether. You can't remove black-swan events from world history, but you can remove them from your finances. How? One very good way is guaranteed-income annuities. Think of annuities as insurance protection against the black swan and against your emotional response to these dark flying creatures.

A Short Catalog of Risk

Black swans represent risk to the extreme, and annuities can be one way to weather those grim storms. Beyond black swans, however, lurking in the bushes are many, many forms of more "normal" risks, all of which—taken separately, or sometimes in combination—can also spill your retirement nest eggs onto the ground.

These risks break down further into

- External risks. These risks from the environment are external to your investments—such as news events or public policy—and generally affect entire markets, but sometimes, as with trade legislation, they can affect specific investments.
- Internal risks. These risks are characteristic of the investment itself, such as competition or poor management decisions, and usually affect single or small similar groups of investments, not entire markets.
- Personal risks. These risks emanate from your own investment habits, practices, and emotions, which can directly affect your portfolio performance.

These risks are ever abundant and prevalent. Some cancel each other out, but all can and will affect your portfolio performance from time to time. Usually we're talking about 5, 10, maybe 20 percent downside risks—not black swans—but these risks can chip away at your worth, particularly if events gang up on you and if you and the rest of the world (the markets) respond to them emotionally.

Anyway, here's my "catalog" of risks to think about as you build and defend your retirement nest egg.

External Risks: The Economic and Event Environment

External risks typically come from governments, economic and political sources, as well as major news or industry events external to specific investments or asset classes.

- Headline risks. These include economic or geopolitical events—like the death or demise of a world leader—that can cause substantial unknowns and uncertainties to the investment climate.
- Policy risks. These usually include deliberate or intended acts of government agencies, such as environmental regulation or the Federal Reserve raising interest rates, that can bring specific effects or add unknowns to the environment.
- Input risks. These risks, like an oil or commodity shortage, can affect individual investments or the economy as a whole as we saw in 1974, 1980, and other times. More important,

in many cases, supply shocks and shortages can affect the perceptions of our economic future.

- Interest rate risk. This is big enough to be called out separately—rate changes or perceptions of rate changes can stimulate or dampen markets considerably and for lengthy periods.
- Inflation risk. This type of risk is almost self-explanatory. Moderate inflation is good because it keeps the economy going, but it will also erode your savings, particularly if you are oriented to fixed-income investments. But the real risk is a rise—or worse, a spike—in inflation rates. Not only does your purchasing power erode, but the perception of higher inflation can be a self-fulfilling prophecy; the cycle is hard to break, as we found in 1979–80.
- Supply chain risks. These are a bit more esoteric and tend to affect some industries more than others. Disruptions in transportation networks (such as port strikes) or the demise of key channel players (like bookstores if you're invested in publishing) can disrupt your investments.
- Financial market risks. Again, these are fairly self-explanatory. Few assets are priced at their intrinsic value; rather, their value is based on what a market perceives them to be worth, whether stocks, gold, real estate, or anything else. As we found out big time in 2008–9, those perceptions can change drastically as financial markets implode, again hitting our investments hard.
- Technology risks. These are more subtle but can disrupt companies, entire industries, or even the economy. Railroads were disrupted by trucking and jet aircraft, radio was disrupted by television, word processors were disrupted by PCs, and more recently, PCs were disrupted by tablets. More globally, the Internet disrupted everything—you get the idea. Not only can such changes disrupt, but they are happening more frequently and faster—no investor (not even Warren Buffett) can ignore the effects and risks brought on by technology change.

Internal Risks: Specific to Your Investment

Risks that might undermine the specific company or fund that you are invested in are internal risks. Obviously bad news or bad performance can affect specific companies, but it can also affect industries or sectors of the economy (like an airline strike). You can minimize but not avoid them completely by avoiding individual stocks and choosing stock or even bond funds instead.

Internal risks include

- News and event risks. The best way to explain is by example: If you're invested in a drug or medical device maker and the Food and Drug Administration declines approval of a new drug or device you're trying to bring to market, that news affects your company directly. These risks are natural for the kind of business these companies are in. Railroads face derailments, airlines may have a crash, and either or both may face new safety regulations—these are good examples of news and event risks specific to a company or its industry.
- Product risks. These are closely related to news and event risks. If you're a medical device maker marketing a new stent and it is found to fail after installation, suddenly you have a big legal and financial headache in the form of recalls, lost market share, brand prestige, and so on. Any company marketing a product or service faces such risks.
- Marketplace risks. Anyone who invested in Research In Motion, creators of the Blackberry, in 2004 knows this one. Your company was king of the hill in the lucrative mobile smartphone environment. It was the prestige standard—everybody wanted one. Then along came the iPhone, and the rest is history. The marketplace can throw all sorts of competitive and technology risks at a company. Nothing is forever, especially these days.
- Operational risks. These risks again include a wide range of perils—a plant fire or safety issue, a strike—anything that throws a wrench in a smooth and oiled production process or supply chain.

- Financial risks. Companies take on risks just as you might by borrowing money or by making other financial commitments that might not work out. As we all know, debt can be a double-edged sword. If financial risk is high and something else goes wrong, the combined effect can be magnified and even lead to bankruptcy.
- Management risks. If you're investing in a company or even a fund, it is managed by people. People make mistakes—and worse, they may have dark and nefarious motives. Although perhaps less common these days, whole companies have imploded on account of bad decisions, unexpected departures, or dastardly deeds of their leaders.

Personal Risks: No Such Thing as a Perfect Investor

Nobody can predict the future, so we as investors start out with a fatal flaw from the get-go. But beyond that, habits, psychology, greed, fear, egos, inattention, and a host of other "human" factors make it hard to get out of our own way sometimes so far as our investments are concerned. No matter how hard you try, no matter how much help you get, and no matter how lucky you are, investing your retirement portfolio is fraught with personal risks.

- Insufficient knowledge. No matter how hard we try, it is simply impossible to know everything about the business, industry, or security we are investing in. We all do research to know what we can, then inevitably leave some of it to faith and instinct—which is, of course, where the gremlins come in.
- Insufficient time. This is a close cousin of insufficient knowledge—we simply don't have the time to research and make the most informed investing decisions. This is where professional help in the form of individual financial advisors or fund managers comes in. But that brings a separate set of risks. In the case of individual advisors, you need to make time to work with them, ask the right questions, and understand the answers as well.
- Emotional override. Our emotional nature tends to magnify risks already present. No matter how logical we think

we are, surprises and volatility make us afraid and can cloud our thinking. Worse, our egos (particularly, our male egos, as independent research has confirmed) can cause us to put blinders on and miss important clues telling us that things have changed and it's time to adjust. Emotional override risk comes in many flavors, but two are worth highlighting:

    - Greed and fear. These manifest themselves in many ways. We tend to think we're invincible when things are going up and overly vulnerable when things are going down. Both lead to bad investment decisions.
    - Failure to accept failure. "I know it will come back" and "It has to get better" are mantras of the emotional investor married to an investment. Our natural tendency as human beings is to think we're right about everything—even as abundant clues surface that say otherwise.

- Not knowing when or how to sell. For most investors, selling is harder than buying. There is a tendency want to hold on to an investment out of fear of missing out on something or to sell something too early in a knee-jerk overreaction to a noncritical event. This causes investors to make a lot of mistakes. "Sell when there's something better to buy (including cash)" is an effective mantra, but most of us still have trouble selling when it makes the most logical sense.
- Cognitive decline. You may be in the best of health, both physically and mentally, as you prepare for retirement and most likely for the first few years of your retirement. But what happens when your cognitive health and ability start to decline? What happens to your investment decisions when your cognitive health and ability decline? The problem here, of course, is not only the loss of cognitive ability but the failure to perceive that your cognitive ability isn't what it used to be. All of a sudden you start making bad decisions and you don't know why, or you do know why and stubbornly refuse to give in to the manifestations of time. Cognitive decline can be one of the biggest risks to your investments during retirement.

- Liability risk. While this applies mainly to taxable investment accounts, assets you own are at risk if you are judged personally liable for an injury or other so-called tort. In many states, annuities typically can shelter you from such liability exposure.

> Risk can undermine your investments, particularly stock investments.
>
> There are many kinds of risk, including external, internal, and personal risks.
>
> Cognitive decline can be one of the biggest—and most silent—risks to your investments.

The Battle Against Volatility and Risk: How to Turn Your Savings into a Guarantee

Wow! What a list! If you take this long list of risks literally, shouldn't you just stuff your cash—or maybe gold coins—under your mattress? Well, there are risks in doing that, too, including the fact that you'll miss out on investment returns and growth.

What to do? With so many risks, how can we ever feel safe enough to retire (or sleep at night if we're already retired)? How do we avoid—or reduce, anyway—our exposure to this daunting list?

Time Out for Defense

As you might have guessed if you've been following my thesis throughout, annuities can help you play defense against such multitudinous investment risks.

As I've suggested, and will cover in detail later on in part 2, annuities can (1) guarantee an income stream for life and (2) protect you against the volatilities and risks of the investment markets.

I recommend protecting some—not all—of your nest egg this way. As we'll discuss, you should keep some of your savings in the markets to participate in growth and provide a cushion for unexpected expenses. But full exposure to these risks is gone forever if you put a portion of that nest egg into annuities.

I should note that most annuities don't get you away from inflation risk, and there is a slight risk—which I'll also cover—of insurance company insolvency. This hasn't actually happened in such a way as to affect an annuity in many years—never in the 21-year history of fixed indexed annuities as I'll describe in part 2. Additionally, as I'll describe in chapter 9, state guaranty associations provide some protection. But it should be noted, so I noted it.

Once again, the sources of volatility and risk are numerous and unavoidable. Fixed and fixed indexed annuities can provide a safe harbor against these disruptive forces and should be considered for a portion of retirement savings, particularly in the few years leading up to or once you reach retirement.

The sources of volatility and risk are numerous and unavoidable.

Fixed and fixed indexed annuities should be considered to "inoculate" your savings against volatility and risk, particularly once you reach retirement.

By the Numbers

- **11.41**. The average percent gain in the S&P 500 1928–2015, including inflation and dividends
- **5.23**. The average percent gain in intermediate-term Treasuries 1928–2015, including interest
- **7.23**. The average percent S&P 500 gain since 2006
- **3.5**. The average percent S&P 500 gain since 2000
- **4.71**. The average intermediate Treasuries gain since 2006
- **15**. The number of years the S&P 500 gained between 0 and 10 percent since 1928 (17 percent of the years elapsed)
- **27**. The number of losing S&P 500 years since 1928 (31 percent)

CHAPTER 7

SAVINGS AND SAFETY, PART 2

Timing Can Be Everything

Guess what? Your hard-earned nest egg—so necessary to save to fill out your retirement plan—is vulnerable. Vulnerable to risk and volatility, as I illustrated in chapter 6. Vulnerable to the market's hard twists and turns, any of which can knock the pins out from under your investments.

That in itself is probably not a surprise. You know that investments, especially in today's markets, are vulnerable to the many speed bumps that lie in wait.

Those ups and downs are bad enough. But there's something else, another "gotcha" in the grand scheme of managing your retirement savings: Not only can basic forms of risk and volatility dump your nest eggs on the ground; the *timing* of those sour market events can also wreak havoc on your savings performance.

To repeat: Beyond risk and volatility themselves, bad timing of market swings, or even unfortunate timing of your actual retirement date to begin with, can also sack your hard-earned retirement savings. If you're unlucky enough to retire during a market slump—or are *forced* into retirement during that slump—your best-laid retirement plans could be in trouble.

Many learned this the hard way with the dot-com crash of 2001 and the Great Recession–leading market crash of 2008–9. Anyone retiring in those years or shortly before saw their invested nest eggs take a 20 to 50 percent haircut or more, depending on how they were invested.

Now, it's a major challenge to earn decent investing returns any time. But trying to make up a 40 percent loss? Given how much of a gain it takes to make up a 40 percent loss (67 percent, as you'll see in a second)? And all after you're already retired? Yikes, that's a tall order.

As we'll see in this chapter, the timing of an investment loss can have a devastating effect on your retirement prospects. A sour market at the outset can spill your nest egg. Not to mix metaphors, but bad timing can dig a hole you may never get out of.

Timing can be everything. Even if you recover the principal, bad timing will affect your returns. It will affect what you can withdraw from you savings during the course of retirement.

You can't control the timing of the ups and downs of the markets. You can't even control exactly when you'll retire—for a variety of reasons, your retirement date may pick you instead of you picking it! The stakes are high here.

So how can you deflect the ravages of bad timing? One good way is to include annuities in your retirement plan. Guaranteed-income annuities are an important way to sidestep timing risks for a portion of your retirement portfolio. With guaranteed-income annuities, timing risk can be transformed from a matter of good or bad luck into a matter of being prepared.

I'll start out by sharing just how hard it is to climb out of a hole once dug, and then I will walk you through a few comparative examples to illustrate the hazards of having a retirement plan dinged at the outset.

Getting Out of a Deep Hole: Gains Required to Recover a Loss

Simple math tells us it's much harder to get out of a hole than to dig one—at least so far as your investments are concerned.

For example, suppose you start with a $1,000 investment. Everything's going fine—then your investment takes a big hit. Whether from external, internal, or personal risks (from chapter 6), it doesn't much matter why, your investment loses $500, or 50 percent of its value.

Now, what needs to happen for you to recover this lost value? Earn a 50 percent return to offset the 50 percent loss? It would seem so—and that would be bad enough. But unfortunately, it doesn't work that way, and the reality is far worse.

To recover a 50 percent investment loss, you have to earn a *100 percent return* on your remaining investment *just to break even.* Double your money. A "two-bagger." Ouch. Now, just what investment strategy is tuned to get you a 100 percent return? Gasp! You're in a deep hole, one that will likely take years to climb out from.

Thankfully, investments don't lose 50 percent very often. Most losses are smaller, but the 50 percent catastrophe makes the point: If your investments lose value, you must not only reverse the fall but invest even more productively to recover the shortfall. And typically, the investment returns required to recover far exceed the modest returns available in today's markets.

How Much Gain to Relieve the Pain?

So how much of a gain does it take to recover from a given loss? As you can see in table 7.1, it takes only an 11 percent gain to recover a 10 percent loss. Not so bad, especially given the historic 11.4 percent average annual gain in the markets (including dividends).

But note what happens when the hole is dug deeper. It takes a 25 percent gain to recover a 20 percent loss, a 43 percent gain to recover a 30 percent loss, and so on.

TABLE 7.1. Gain Required to Make Up a Loss

Loss (%)	Gain Required (%)
−10	11
−20	25
−30	43
−40	67
−50	100
−60	150
−70	233
−80	400
−90	900

Again, it's important to realize just how good you'll have to be as an investor to recover from a bad period. Gains of 25 to 50 percent—let alone 100 percent—are pretty darned hard to find.

In fact, what's likely to happen as we normal human beings fall into the "emotional override" trap (chapter 6 again) is that we try harder; we put more chips on the table to recover the loss and recover it quickly.

We all know what happens when we fall into that natural trap of human nature: We lose more. The hole gets deeper. It's more likely to go to zero (or something close) than recover our investment once this cycle starts. Unless, of course, we're lucky.

And the point, once again, that I'm trying to hammer home is that you won't lose 10, 20, 30, or any percent if you have some money safely invested in a fixed or fixed indexed annuity. You'll never have to face the prospect of having to generate double- and even triple-digit returns just to get your nest egg back.

> When you're invested in fixed or fixed indexed annuities, you'll never have to face earning double- or even triple-digit market gains just to get your nest egg back.

Up, Down, Sideways: It's All in the Timing

Now you have a pretty good grasp on the idea that even a small correction or bear market can put you in a fairly deep hole. When you invest for retirement, your first hope is to preserve your capital so that you can withdraw from it in an orderly fashion at a pace that gives you what you need without depleting it too fast.

Your second hope—the Holy Grail—is to actually grow your capital so that your retirement needs are funded by the growth and returns rather than by depleting your capital. You want to live off the golden eggs, not the goose. We all do.

So you can see just how far from this ideal you can find yourself if your savings are dinged right off the bat.

Pathways to Failure and Success: Three Paths to 20 Years of Retirement

Timing can be everything, and the best way to demonstrate that is to show four retirement scenarios. In each of the four scenarios, the starting retirement savings amounts are the same and the markets end up where they started. "So what's the diff?" you might fairly ask. How can your retirement be affected by an investment pot that starts and ends the same?

It's all about timing. Depending on when the markets take a hit and/or recover during those the 20 years, your retirement payout can vary a great deal. Gain early and your investments will compound faster and throw off more income. Lose early and your investments will be in recovery mode and will throw off less income—sometimes quite a bit less.

Thus, in these three scenarios, the income produced is far different depending on what happened to the markets during the retirement period. The savings principal left over at the end of the retirement period may differ as well.

The three scenarios I show are 20 years in length, start with $100,000 in savings (not much, but easy to make calculations), and support a 4 percent annual withdrawal to help fund your retirement. (I'll cover the so-called 4 percent rule in more depth in the next chapter on retirement planning models.)

The basic theme is to discover what happens (1) when the markets exhibit normal volatility, (2) when the markets start out with gains and follow with losses to revert to their starting point, and (3) when the market start out with losses and follow with gains to revert to their starting point.

Normal Ebb and Flow: Steady-State Returns

Markets go up, markets go down. In the simplest scenario, that's all that happens. The markets stay the same but go up and down around a given level. Normal and normally distributed volatility would give ups and downs in an orderly and evenly distributed pattern throughout the years.

Table 7.2 shows a 20-year retirement savings scenario where returns alternate around 0 percent: down 5 percent the first two years, up 5 percent the next two, down 5 percent the next two, and so forth.

TABLE 7.2. Retirement Scenario #1: Steady-State Returns

20-Year Retirement, 4% Annual Withdrawals					
Alternating +5%, −5% Returns					
Initial Amount ($)	Year	Annual Return (%)	Year-End Total Before Withdrawal ($)	4% Withdrawal ($)	Year-End Total After Withdrawal ($)
100,000	1	−5	95,000	3,800	91,200
	2	−5	86,640	3,466	83,174
	3	+5	87,333	3,493	83,840
	4	+5	88,032	3,521	84,511
	5	−5	80,285	3,211	77,074
	6	−5	73,220	2,929	70,291
	7	+5	73,806	2,952	70,853
	8	+5	74,396	2,976	71,420
	9	−5	67,849	2,714	65,135
	10	−5	61,879	2,475	59,403
	11	+5	62,374	2,495	59,879
	12	+5	62,873	2,515	60,358
	13	−5	57,340	2,294	55,046
	14	−5	52,294	2,092	50,202
	15	+5	52,712	2,108	50,604
	16	+5	53,134	2,125	51,009
	17	−5	48,458	1,938	46,520
	18	−5	44,194	1,768	42,426
	19	+5%	$44,547	$1,782	$ 42,765
	20	+5%	$44,904	$1,796	$ 43,108
		Total Withdrawn		$52,451	
		Ending Amount			$43,108

In this base case, the savings balance declines slowly as savings are withdrawn but gets pumped up a bit in positive years. Withdrawals—based on the fixed 4 percent of the savings balance—decay slowly as well. The total withdrawn plus the ending amount roughly equal what was put in and would slightly exceed the initial amount if the first two years' returns were positive.

The Early Returns Are Positive

Table 7.2 shows a pretty calm scenario over the 20 years, but as I pointed out in the last chapter, markets have a tendency, especially these days, to *not* settle for modest 5 percent annual gains and losses.

Instead, they tend to go through longer periods of consecutive loss (2008–10) and gain (2011–15). So what happens if you retire right in front of one of these gain or loss periods? Tables 7.3 and 7.4 show us.

Table 7.3 shows the rosy scenario where you start your retirement and then the markets go gangbusters, racking up a pretty unrealistic 10 straight years of 10 percent gains, followed by 10 straight years of 10 percent losses. Gain, gain, gain, then loss, loss, loss.

What happens? The principal grows at first, generating more gains as return on principal and throwing off more cash as the 4 percent withdrawals are taken.

TABLE 7.3. Retirement Scenario #2: The Effect of Early Gains

20-Year Retirement, 4% Annual Withdrawals					
Positive Returns, First 10 Years					
Initial Amount ($)	Year	Annual Return (%)	Year-End Total Before Withdrawal ($)	4% Withdrawal ($)	Year-End Total After Withdrawal ($)
100,000	1	+10	110,000	4,400	105,600
	2	+10	116,160	4,646	111,514
	3	+10	122,665	4,907	117,758
	4	+10	129,534	5,181	124,353
	5	+10	136,788	5,472	131,317
	6	+10	144,448	5,778	138,670
(*continued*)					

(*continued*)					
Initial Amount ($)	Year	Annual Return (%)	Year-End Total Before Withdrawal ($)	4% Withdrawal ($)	Year-End Total After Withdrawal ($)
	7	+10	152,537	6,101	146,436
	8	+10	161,079	6,443	154,636
	9	+10	170,100	6,804	163,296
	10	+10	179,625	7,185	172,440
	11	−10	155,196	6,208	148,989
	12	−10	134,090	5,364	128,726
	13	−10	115,854	4,634	111,219
	14	−10	100,097	4,004	96,094
	15	−10	86,484	3,459	83,025
	16	−10	74,722	2,989	71,733
	17	−10	64,560	2,582	61,978
	18	−10	55,780	2,231	53,549
	19	−10	48,194	1,928	46,266
	20	−10	41,639	1,666	39,974
		Total Withdrawn		91,982	
		Ending Amount			39,974

Even though this scenario, like the others, puts the markets right back where they started, the early strong gains build the retirement account and allow it to throw off far more cash, $91,982 in withdrawals versus $52,451 in the "steady state" scenario in table 7.2. That's almost $40,000 in extra withdrawals on a $100,000 base just because gains came in early in the withdrawal period.

Starting Out on the Downside

The real contrast, and a main point of this exercise, is between the scenario presented in table 7.3 and the one presented in table 7.4—that is, the difference between a scenario of large up-front gains versus large up-front losses.

Consider table 7.4, where the markets and savings portfolio loses 10 percent for each of the first 10 years and then gains that amount over the last 10—again to break even at the end of 20 years.

TABLE 7.4. Retirement Scenario #3: The Effect of Early Losses

20-Year Retirement, 4% Annual Withdrawals					
Negative Returns, First 10 Years					
Initial Amount ($)	Year	Annual Return (%)	Year-End Total Before Withdrawal ($)	4% Withdrawal ($)	Year-End Total After Withdrawal ($)
100,000	1	−10	90,000	3,600	86,400
	2	−10	77,760	3,110	74,650
	3	−10	67,185	2,687	64,497
	4	−10	58,048	2,322	55,726
	5	−10	50,153	2,006	48,147
	6	−10	43,332	1,733	41,599
	7	−10	37,439	1,498	35,941
	8	−10	32,347	1,294	31,053
	9	−10	27,948	1,118	26,830
	10	−10	24,147	966	23,181
	11	+10	25,499	1,020	24,479
	12	+10	26,927	1,077	25,850
	13	+10	28,435	1,137	27,298
	14	+10	30,028	1,201	28,827
	15	+10	31,709	1,268	30,441
	16	+10	33,485	1,339	32,146
	17	+10	35,360	1,414	33,946
	18	+10	37,340	1,494	35,847
	19	+10	39,431	1,577	37,854
	20	+10	41,639	1,666	39,974
		Total Withdrawn		33,529	
		Ending Amount			39,974

The interesting point is to note that since the markets ended up right back where they started, the ending balances in the early gain scenario (table 7.3) and the late-gain scenario (table 7.4) are identical, at $39,974. However, the diminished balance in the early years of the late-gain scenario ends up funding far smaller withdrawals, so the total withdrawn in this scenario is $33,529—almost $60,000 less than the rosy scenario in table 7.3 where the gains came early ($91,982)!

Early Hits Hit Hard

You can see how timing can be everything. For a more realistic example—one that resembles 2001–2 or 2008–9—I'll show one final scenario where the markets take a 20 percent hit in each of the first two years after an imagined retirement. After that, they stabilize and enter a steady state, alternating the 5 percent gains and losses I showed in the first scenario.

TABLE 7.5. Retirement Scenario #4: Early Hits Hit Hard

20-Year Retirement, 4% Annual Withdrawals					
−20% Returns, First Two Years					
Initial Amount ($)	Year	Annual Return (%)	Year-End Total Before Withdrawal (%)	4% Withdrawal ($)	Year-End Total After Withdrawal ($)
100,000	1	−20	80,000	3,200	76,800
	2	−20	61,440	2,458	58,982
	3	+5	61,932	2,477	59,454
	4	+5	62,427	2,497	59,930
	5	−5	56,933	2,277	54,656
	6	−5	51,923	2,077	49,846
	7	+5	52,339	2,094	50,245
	8	+5	52,757	2,110	50,647
	9	−5	48,115	1,925	46,190
	10	−5	43,881	1,755	42,125
	11	+5	44,232	1,769	42,462
	12	+5	44,586	1,783	42,802
(continued)					

TABLE 7.5. Retirement Scenario #4: Early Hits Hit Hard *(continued)*					
20-Year Retirement, 4% Annual Withdrawals					
−20% Returns, First Two Years					
Initial Amount ($)	Year	Annual Return (%)	Year-End Total Before Withdrawal (%)	4% Withdrawal ($)	Year-End Total After Withdrawal ($)
	13	−5	40,662	1,626	39,036
	14	−5	37,084	1,483	35,600
	15	+5	37,380	1,495	35,885
	16	+5	37,679	1,507	36,172
	17	−5	34,364	1,375	32,989
	18	−5	31,340	1,254	30,086
	19	+5	31,590	1,264	30,327
	20	+5	31,843	1,274	30,569
		Total Withdrawn		37,700	
		Ending Amount			30,569

Note again that both the total withdrawals and the ending amount take a hit in this scenario. The total of withdrawals and ending balance fall far short of the initial $100,000 investment, and this combined total ($66,289) even falls somewhat short of the combined total ($73,503) after 20 years in the scenario in table 7.4, where losses were endured for 10 straight years! Of course, it falls well short of the "steady state" table 7.2 scenario.

The bottom line is this: Sour markets at the beginning of a retirement period spell trouble—take note.

The Battle Against Bad Timing: How to Turn Your Savings into a Guarantee

The point of showing these scenarios should be obvious: It isn't just about *whether* the markets gain or lose during your retirement; it's about *when* they gain or lose as well. People who retired in 2000–2001 or 2007–8 know this well. It's heartbreaking to take a sound nest egg into retirement only to have the markets drop early, reducing your withdrawals, sometimes dramatically, and making you play catch-up throughout your retirement.

You can do something about this! You can choose not to protect yourself from forced retirement and let the markets have their way with you. Or, through proper preparation, you can defend yourself against the vagaries of timing.

There are a number of ways you can protect yourself against doomsday market and retirement-date scenarios. A great means of protection is to put at least some of your retirement nest egg into fixed or fixed indexed annuities, which I'll describe in part 2. These annuities eliminate the risk of an early meltdown during your retirement for the assets deployed in that direction.

Remember, preparation is the best way to deal with uncertainty. You'll be able to sleep at night.

> Early market meltdowns during your retirement period can devastate your retirement withdrawals.
>
> This risk can be reduced by putting some of your savings into guaranteed-income annuities.
>
> As in all matters of uncertainty, preparation is the key.

By the Numbers

- **100.** The percent gain on your investments to recover a 50 percent loss
- **43.** The percent gain on your investments to recover a 30 percent loss
- **37.** The percent "hit" your withdrawals will take if the markets lose 10 percent in the first 10 years versus a "steady state" scenario ($33,529 vs. $52,451)
- **64.** The percent "hit" your withdrawals will take over 20 years if the markets lose 10 percent in the first 10 years versus gaining 10 percent the first 10 years ($33,529 vs. $91,982)

CHAPTER 8

CALCULATING YOUR RETIREMENT

Simple Math Goes a Long Way

If you're a number-cruncher, then you'll love this chapter. But if you're not, don't worry too much if you're not interested in the formulas. The calculations here are meant to help you determine how much you'll need from each source of funds for your retirement.

Retirement savings. The most dynamic, and for most, the most critical pillar of a retirement plan. Sure, there's Social Security, but it isn't enough. Then, if you're lucky, there's a pension. Beyond that, you need savings: Savings to fill the gap, savings to provide a steady stream of income, and a reserve for extraordinary purchases and expenses.

The bottom line is that while much is typically expected of your savings, they're exposed to a lot of perils and hazards—particularly as described in chapters 6 and 7. I've put it out there as a major thesis of this book that annuities can remove some of the perils and hazards in favor of a guaranteed income stream for life.

I've left one question uncovered (aside from the detailed explanation of annuities, which I'll get to in part 2)—that is, how much savings do you need? Whether converted into an annuity or not, what "number" will give you access to the income you need in retirement? What are you shooting for?

The answer, of course, requires some calculation. It requires quantifying your retirement income needs, your longevity, and your current resources. Basically, it gets down to calculating the "gap" between your Social Security (and perhaps pension) payments and what you actually need to retire.

The trouble is, those calculations can be complex. You will need to consider many scenarios, factor in many variables, and coordinate many moving parts to get to that number. The moving parts include, but aren't limited to, longevity, investment returns, investment "compounding," market volatility, spousal needs and resources, housing needs, care and "hired-out" needs, and irregular items like inheritances, business sales, new roofs, or unexpected medical expenses.

It's hard—no, really, it's impossible—to come up with a model, a "black box" that precisely covers everything. And yet, many models try to do it all! They try to forecast every detail with more precision than what's really feasible or even possible. The nature and variability of the unknowns is simply too great. Some models suggest precise answers, but they cannot really be that precise. They lose the forest for the trees! And often, you can't understand the answer anyhow.

As a consequence, I prefer simple models. I will describe three such models in this chapter: (1) the "4 percent rule," (2) the accumulation and distribution annuity model, and (3) the relatively simple, easy-to-use calculator available online called the Ultimate Retirement Calculator.

The 4 Percent Rule

Although it has come under some criticism in recent years as a result of today's low interest rates, the "4 percent rule" is simplest of all.

Assuming your savings are invested to generate a moderate return, you can afford to withdraw 4 percent of your retirement savings each year with very little chance of depleting your savings through a 30-year retirement. How do we know? Because the rule has been tested against 67 years of actual history—albeit market and fixed income returns have been higher most of those years than they are now.

Here's how it works.

First off, the arithmetic is basic—if you have $1 million saved for retirement, you can safely withdraw $40,000 per year.

Conversely, you can reverse the equation: If you need $40,000 a year in dependable pretax income from your savings, you need to have $1 million saved.

Naturally, the amount of income you need from savings does not include Social Security or other entitlements; if you get $24,000 from Social Security as well, your savings will bring you up to $64,000 per year, which may render some or all of your Social Security benefits taxable (see chapter 5).

Now, what could be simpler than that? Just plug in your annual income "gap" and multiply by 25 (100 percent divided by 4 percent)! You've got your number.

Some people refer to the 4 percent rule as a spending plan tool, a calculation of how much you can spend in a year. I like to take it a step further—to help determine the nest egg necessary on Retirement Day One to support your annual spending.

Basic Rule and Origin

The 4 percent rule comes from empirical research done in 1993 by certified financial planner (CFP®) William Bengen.

Bengen experimented with different withdrawal rates against actual market performance in every 30 year period since 1926 (67 years). He found that if you withdrew 4 percent each year, you would not have run out of money in *any* of the observed 30-year periods since then (although some of them are still not complete).

Here are a few more fun facts about the rule:

- You can actually increase the initial withdrawal by the inflation rate every year. So if $4,000 was withdrawn in the first year from a $100,000 nest egg and the inflation rate for the previous year was 2 percent, the withdrawal could be expanded to $4,080 in the second year. (Why? Because the value of your stock or stock-based investments grows accordingly with inflation.)
- The model assumes you're invested in 50 percent US stocks as represented by the S&P 500 and 50 percent intermediate-term government bonds. Any other

investment allocation—either more or less risky—could violate the rule.

- The rule assumes that your portfolio is rebalanced each year to get to preserve the 50/50 allocation. So if stocks are up in a given year, some are sold to buy more bonds to get back to that ratio.
- Stock and bond index funds are reasonable choices to invest in to achieve the allocation.
- You are a buy-and-hold investor—that is, except for rebalancing the portfolio annually, you don't buy and sell to try to time the market.
- Withdrawals are taken at the beginning of the year.
- Dividends and interest are reinvested and are withdrawn only as part of scheduled withdrawals.

> The 4 percent rule suggests that your nest egg can support a 4 percent withdrawal every year with little chance of running out of cash.
>
> You can "turn around" the 4 percent rule to estimate your required nest egg: Multiply your desired yearly income from savings by 25 (1 divided by 0.04).

Tweaking the Assumptions

The 4 percent rule has been energetically tweaked and tested since its initial 1993 conception. It's fair to ask whether the 4 percent rule still even holds true with today's low bond yields and more volatile markets. That has been researched, as have different withdrawal rates under different investment strategies and variable withdrawal rates depending on market performance.

Here are some variations researchers have come up with:

- *More aggressive investing.* Bengen himself in 1998 did some work to find out what would happen if 25 percent of the total portfolio (half the stock portfolio) was invested in smaller, more aggressive stocks. He found that the greater growth and volatility actually support a 4.5 percent withdrawal rate with 30-year safety.

- *Moderated withdrawals in bad years.* Financial planner Jonathan Guyton noted that the 4 percent rule worked even for the three worst 30-year periods (starting 1929, 1937, and 1973) and wondered what would happen if withdrawals were moderated slightly. He postulated that if withdrawals were moderated by 10 percent in the bad years (a reasonable belt tightening for most), the withdrawal rate could be increased to 5.5 percent.
- *Variable withdrawal rates depending on market performance.* Researcher and financial advisor Michael Kitces tested what would happen if withdrawal rates were moderated depending on market valuation. A withdrawal rate of 4 to 4.5 percent in overvalued markets (market or S&P 500 total P/E >20, based on 10 years' earnings), 5 percent in fairly valued markets (P/E between 12 and 20) and 5.5 percent in undervalued markets (P/E <12) worked well.
- *Today's environment: 3 percent?* With today's low interest rates and overvalued markets, retirement expert and professor Wade Pfau suggests moderating the initial rate to 3 percent if at all possible and raising it gradually as markets return to more historic norms. Recent studies have suggested even higher portfolio "failure rates" at today's levels of interest rates and returns, so a safe 3 percent withdrawal assumption or even lower might be prudent.

> Depending on your assumptions, risk tolerance, and willingness to be flexible with withdrawals, a lump sum can support withdrawals ranging from 3 to 5.5 percent.
>
> Conservative investors and planners might use a lower withdrawal assumption in today's environment based on today's low interest rates.

> Fixed and fixed indexed annuities can often generate higher payouts, and have less risk of failure, than the 4 percent rule in today's environment.

Using the Rule

The rule, and all of its scenarios, suggest withdrawal rates between 3 and 5.5 percent depending on current conditions and risk tolerance. With traditional assumptions, for modeling purposes they all center on 4 to 4.5 percent, which again makes sense as a denominator to plan your overall nest egg needs. Again, in today's environment, you probably should use a lower withdrawal rate assumption, which as a denominator will in turn increase the lump sums you will need to plan for.

Strengths and Weaknesses

The 4 percent rule has been a good rule of thumb, a good quick calculator to figure a nest egg amount and the annual withdrawals it supports. It is simple, reliable (so far, no black swan has yet to defeat it), and robust. But there are some downsides:

- There is a greater chance of failure at today's lower interest and return rates.
- You might live longer than 30 years in retirement (the rule only covers 30 years).
- Black swan market events or persistent low interest rates can deliver results worse than any of the previous 30-year periods.
- Those "worse results" could conspire to happen right in the beginning of your retirement (see the effect in chapter 7).
- Taxes aren't considered, so what you really need to withdraw might be greater depending on your tax situation.

Annuities Versus the 4 Percent Rule

You might wonder, if the 4 percent rule were "guaranteed" safe—at least as tested against history—why would you ever choose an annuity?

There are four compelling reasons an annuity could be better than simply withdrawing 4 percent (or 4.5 percent or higher) annually:

1. *Lower returns.* If the recent shift toward lower interest rates and returns is permanent, the 4 percent rule is more prone to failure.
2. *Longevity.* You (or your spouse) might live longer than 30 years. The 4 percent rule has only been tested for 30-year periods. Most annuities cover forever.
3. *Black swans.* The 4 percent rule has only been tested against what has happened since 1926. What if something worse than that happened? An annuity is guaranteed and would protect against a black swan.
4. *Insurance pooling.* Many fixed and fixed indexed annuities can generate a higher payout annually depending on a number of factors, including the age where payouts begin. How can they do this if a "guaranteed" return tests out to only 4 percent or less in the rule? It's because, as with most insurance products, your annuity is pooled with many other annuity holders. Some of them die before the actuarially expected number of years, leaving funds with the annuity provider that can be distributed among other annuity holders.

I should once again note annuity downsides too: You pay fees on many annuities, which must be compared to fees up front and annually on other traditional investments. Too, the "black swan" of an annuity seller's bankruptcy sits out there somewhere—the guarantee isn't *absolutely* perfect.

Those facts given, a savings strategy that combines purchased annuities with standard savings subject to 3 to 5.5 percent annual withdrawals can make a lot of sense. In light of the recent return environment, guaranteed annuities (fixed and fixed indexed) are becoming more attractive.

And, once again, the 4 percent rule can be worked backward to estimate a nest egg sufficient to meet the retirement income "gap."

> Annuities can be a sound alternative to the 4 percent rule. They sidestep the risk of lower market and fixed income returns, eliminate most black swans, can pay out longer than 30 years, and pool many investors—some of whom die early—to distribute relatively more income per dollar invested to surviving annuity holders.

Annuity Math: A Slightly Less Simple Approach to Finding Your Number

This book is about planning for retirement and, as might be kind of obvious by now, how to use annuities to help with that plan.

Annuities, as we will soon see, are products sold mostly by insurance companies that guarantee a future income stream in return for an up-front payment. The up-front payment is collected either as a lump sum or as installments to reach a set amount of funds when the annuity payments start. The annuity payments are distributed periodically, commonly annually or monthly, usually but not always for a lifetime (or multiple lifetimes, if survivor benefits are sought).

Two big questions come to mind: How much lump sum up front does it take to generate a certain desired payment? Or, given a certain lump sum up front, how big of a "payment" can you receive?

These questions can be answered by "annuity math." Annuity math is based on the principles of compounding math, which I'll describe now.

(Uh-oh, here we go—*math.* Yuck. I promise this won't be so bad and that the true "math" will be done for you when we get to the point of calculating your lump sum. Have faith . . . it's not *that* bad. *Promise!*)

A Wee Bit of Compounding Math

Compounding math measures the growth of a sum of money over a given period of time, at a given return rate, where both the original sum and the returns earned are left to grow by that return rate. Mathematically, a future value (FV) equals a present value (PV) compounded for a number of years (n) at an annual return rate of (i).

The formula—and I promise nothing more complex—is

$$\mathbf{FV = PV * (1 + i)^n}$$

So if you have a lump sum of $1,000 invested at 5 percent for 10 years, the formula looks like this:

$$\mathbf{FV = \$1{,}000 * (1 + .05)^{10}}$$

or

$$\mathbf{FV = \$1{,}000 * (1.05)^{10}}$$

or

$$\mathbf{FV = \$1{,}000 * (1.629)}$$

or

$$\mathbf{\$1{,}629}$$

What's really happening here? You're earning a return on your original investment plus a return on each year's returns. These returns on returns can add up considerably over the years.

Note that without compounding, your 5 percent return would produce $50 in income each year—for 10 years, that would add up to $500 as a total return. With compounding, you earn $629 because the returns earn a return as well. Very small increments in either *i* (the return rate) or *n* (the number of years) can add up to huge numbers, as you might imagine.

But I'm not here to give math lessons. Nor am I here to amaze you with the power of compounding, which Einstein considered to be the "eighth wonder of the world." I'll leave that to other authors, personal finance show hosts, and others. I'm here (in this chapter, anyway) to provide simple tools to estimate your retirement needs.

From Compounding Math to Annuity Math

Compounding math calculates the future value of a single sum compounded over time. It also can be worked backward to calculate a PV required to grow into a desired FV within a certain time period at a set rate of return.

But what happens when, instead of a single lump sum, you choose to save in installments over time? Your lump sum isn't fixed—it grows over time as you deposit funds, as in saving for retirement. Whatever sum you have in a particular year grows by the return rate and compounds as well. But you aren't starting with a single PV lump sum.

What you have here is a mathematical annuity (as opposed to the insurance product you might buy). It's an annuity because it makes regular payments into the compounding machine.

As you might guess, the math gets a little more complicated. Each year's added sum must be compounded for the number of years left in the time period, and its earnings must be compounded as well.

Yes, the formula is complex. And I'll spare you.

Distribution and Accumulation Annuities

The simple annuity I just described *accumulates* funds over time—say, $1,000 per year instead of just $20,000 up front. It calculates an FV based on the payments, the length of time, and the return rate on the accumulated funds. Thus it's called an *accumulation annuity.*

Now, just as with basic compounding, you can also work backward. You can start with a lump sum and calculate a regular payment *out* of that lump sum, again based on a length of time and the return rate applied to the *remaining* funds. So, if you start with $20,000, how much could be *paid out* each year for *n* years earning a return rate of *i*? The even-more-complex formula—which I again won't share—calculates that annual or monthly amount.

This is a *distribution annuity.* Here, a beginning lump sum supports regular annuity payments for a given period of time at a given return rate. With some subtle differences to accommodate the "longevity guaranteed" nature of annuity *products,* this is the basic math used to do the inner calculations for annuity products I'll soon describe.

It's powerful math and, you guessed it, you can use it to work backward from an income stream you need in retirement to a lump sum required on Retirement Day One.

And guess what else? Once you establish this Day One lump sum, you can deploy the accumulation annuity math to estimate what you have to save per month or per year to *get to* that lump sum.

Now I will show you how to use distribution and accumulation annuities to estimate a lump sum nest egg and how to develop a savings plan to accumulate it. Whew, the math part is over. The rest is simple.

Calculating the Lump Sum Using Distribution Annuity Math

Starting at the beginning, we calculate the necessary Retirement Day One lump sum by working backward from the desired annual income in retirement to a single sum required to provide that annual income "annuity."

That is done with the distribution annuity table (see table 8.1), which shows what annual payment a single dollar supports for a given time at a given return rate.

For example, if you earn 4 percent over 30 years, the factor in the table is 17.3. To arrive at the annual payment that single dollar invested up front can provide, assuming it earns 4 percent, you divide that dollar by 17.3. You get about 5.8 cents. A dollar deposited on Retirement Day One would pay you 5.8 cents annually for 30 years at 4 percent. Without compounding, it would only be 3.3 cents, or $1 divided by 30 years.

Note that the return rate assumption of 4 percent is constant—4 percent every year, no exceptions. The volatility of returns in the real world suggests you should save more than the model recommends.

Of course, you will undoubtedly accumulate more than $1 by Retirement Day One. Suppose you had $300,000 saved. That $300,000, divided by 17.3, would give you approximately $17,341 per year, or $1,445 per month.

Working Backward: The Lump Sum

As I mentioned above, you can work backward, applying the factors in the distribution annuity table to get a lump sum needed on Retirement Day One to support a given desired payment in retirement.

Suppose you decide you need $25,000 annually from your savings for 30 years, and you expect to earn 4 percent on your investments. The factor, once again, is 17.3. But this time you *multiply*—$25,000 times 17.3—giving $432,500 as the amount you need to save by Retirement Day One to support this annual payment.

TABLE 8.1. "Distribution Annuity": Present Value of $1 Distributed per Year (%)

	Number of Years								
Rate of Return (%)		**1**	**2**	**5**	**10**	**15**	**20**	**30**	**40**
	1.0	1.0	2.0	4.9	9.5	13.9	18.0	25.8	32.8
	2.0	1.0	1.9	4.7	9.0	12.8	16.4	22.4	27.4
	3.0	1.0	1.9	4.6	8.5	11.9	14.9	19.6	23.1
	4.0	1.0	1.9	4.5	8.1	11.1	13.6	17.3	19.8
	5.0	1.0	1.9	4.3	7.7	10.4	12.5	15.4	17.2
	6.0	0.9	1.8	4.2	7.4	9.7	11.5	13.8	15.0
	8.0	0.9	1.8	4.0	6.7	8.6	9.8	11.3	11.9
	10.0	0.9	1.7	3.8	6.1	7.6	8.5	9.4	9.8
	12.0	0.9	1.7	3.6	5.7	6.8	7.5	8.1	8.2
	15.0	0.9	1.6	3.4	5.0	5.8	6.3	6.6	6.6
	20.0	0.8	1.5	3.0	4.2	4.7	4.9	5.0	5.0

Distribution annuity math allows you to work backward to a lump sum that would support a given annual payment for a given number of years at a given rate of return.

Why Mutual Funds (and Financial Advice) Can Be So Expensive

Although both mutual fund and asset management fees and charges have been coming down of late, the annuity math I've been describing well illustrates how even a "paltry" 1 percent taken out of your investments by a mutual fund, broker, and/or financial advisor can really be costly.

In the above example, if you're getting 4 percent over 30 years, you need $432,500 on Retirement Day One to pay out $25,000 annually to you over 30 years.

But what happens if we take 1 percent out of your returns to pay these funds and advisors? Now at 3 percent, your distribution annuity factor is 19.6. What lump sum do you need now?

Multiply $25,000 by 19.6 and you get $490,000—you need to save $57,500 more just to cover the costs of your funds and/or advisors!

You can also see from this, aside from fees and expenses, how return rates matter. Invest carefully, but do invest!

Or you can buy an annuity with part of that nest egg once you have it, leaving the driving to someone else.

Building the Lump Sum Using Accumulation Annuity Math

Now that we have the lump sum needed on Retirement Day One ($432,500 in the example), the next, last, and simplest step is to figure out how much must be saved each year during your working years to attain this lump sum.

The math now switches over to the accumulation annuity table, which gives factors by time available to save and return rate to calculate the necessary annual savings (see table 8.2).

TABLE 8.2. "Accumulation Annuity": Future Value of $1 Saved per Year (%)

	Number of Years								
Rate of Return (%)		**1**	**2**	**5**	**10**	**15**	**20**	**30**	**40**
	1.0	1.0	2.0	5.1	10.5	16.1	22.0	34.8	48.9
	2.0	1.0	2.0	5.2	10.9	17.3	24.3	40.6	60.4
	3.0	1.0	2.0	5.3	11.5	18.6	26.9	47.6	75.4
	4.0	1.0	2.0	5.4	12.0	20.0	29.8	56.1	95.0
	5.0	1.0	2.1	5.5	12.6	21.6	33.1	66.4	120.8
	6.0	1.0	2.1	5.6	13.2	23.3	36.8	79.1	154.8
	8.0	1.0	2.1	5.9	14.5	27.2	45.8	113.3	259.1
	10.0	1.0	2.1	6.1	15.9	31.8	57.3	164.5	442.6
	12.0	1.0	2.1	6.4	17.5	37.3	72.1	241.3	767.1
	15.0	1.0	2.2	6.7	20.3	47.6	102.4	434.7	1779.1
	20.0	1.0	2.2	7.4	26.0	72.0	186.7	1181.9	7343.9

Here's how this relatively simple table works: Suppose you have 20 years left as a worker to save. You feel you can earn 5 percent returns. The factor for 20 years at 5 percent is 33.1.

Simply divide $432,500 (the Retirement Day One lump sum) by 33.1, giving $13,066 per year, or a little over $1,000 a month, needed to save to achieve this amount.

It's fun to play "what-if" games with this table. For instance, if you had 30 years instead of 20 to save, the factor rises substantially to 66.4, giving an annual savings required of only $6,514. That's quite a difference for only 10 years more to save. You can see why they say "Start young"!

Similarly, you can see how more conservative investing (or today's lower return rates) requires you to save a lot more. If you get only 3 percent returns on your investments, the 20-year factor drops to 26.9. Now you must save $16,078 a year over 20 years to make your nut. Quite a difference once again!

> Accumulation annuity math allows you to work forward through your working and saving years estimate the annual savings amount needed to accrue a lump sum.

Making It All Work

Once you get used to plugging numbers into your retirement calculations, the distribution/accumulation annuity model becomes quite simple and easy to use. Here's a review:

Step 1. Calculate the lump sum desired for Retirement Day One:

a. Determine the annual payment you desire in retirement.
b. Determine the length of retirement and the return rate you expect.
c. Look up the factor for that time period and return rate on the Distribution Annuity table.
d. Multiply the annual payment by that factor (in our example, $25,000 by 17.3, getting $432,500). That's

your Retirement Day One lump sum for a 30-year retirement at a 4 percent return.

Step 2. Develop a savings plan to get to your Retirement Day One lump sum:

a. Decide how long you have to save and what your return rate will be.
b. Look up the factor on the Accumulation Annuity table.
c. Divide the lump sum by that factor to determine the amount you need to save each year (in our example, $432,500 divided by 33.1, giving $13,066 per year for 20 years, again with a 5 percent return).

Once you get familiar with these tables, they give you the mathematical shorthand and the power to model many possibilities quickly. They also give you visibility into how sensitive your retirement plan is to small and large changes in lifestyle, longevity, savings horizons, and return rates.

And in addition, they give some valuable conceptual understanding of how annuity products can do the work for you.

Comparing Annuity Math and the 4 Percent Rule

As a sharp-eyed reader, you may have noticed an apparent discrepancy between the 4 percent rule and the annuity math calculation just described.

From the text above, a distribution annuity of $432,000 would give you $25,000 annually, assuming an investment return of 4 percent.

From the 4 percent rule, it would take $625,000 to deliver the same result ($625,000 × .04 = $25,000 per year).

What's the difference? Why does one model (the 4 percent rule) suggest a lump sum of $625,000 at Retirement Day One for a 30-year retirement, while annuity math suggests only $432,000?

The answer has to do with uncertainty: The smaller amount calculated using annuity math assumes no risk or volatility to affect the lump sum remaining after withdrawals are taken. Payments are even, and nothing happens to the balance. The

4 percent rule gives an extra implied cushion, based on actual market performance collected empirically, of what could happen to your lump sum in 30 years, implicitly building in the protection.

Different strokes for different folks, but one lesson is that if you use annuity math, you should build something extra in just in case your investments earn less—perhaps far less—than 4 percent in a given year.

This also tells you that you should plan to set aside additional savings for risk and uncertainty—in other words, your retirement will *not* go according to plan. Calculate a "number," then add some.

And by the way, the no-volatility assumption used by the annuity math model emulates the real world for a guaranteed (fixed or fixed indexed) annuity *product*—investment risk is borne by the insurer (the annuity seller), not you.

No extra cushion is required with an annuity, at least for investment risk.

Online Retirement Calculators

Naturally—and as you probably already realize—there are a great many retirement calculators available, mostly online. Online calculators allow you to incorporate a lot of assumptions, and they usually use those assumptions to give you a lump-sum estimate as we've done in the previous sections. T. Rowe Price and Fidelity provide two of the more popular entries into this game.

Many use simulations—a testing of multiple good and bad investment scenarios—to arrive at that lump sum. Some use simulations to predict how confident you can be in your retirement with a given lump sum or a range of lump sums. All are more complicated than the models I've presented in this chapter. All must be learned, and many suffer the fate—as I suggested earlier—of trying to predict something with more precision than is really possible.

I don't want to spend more of your reading time analyzing, comparing, and contrasting the myriad models out there. However, they are useful, and I do encourage you to explore them.

I will, however, briefly share one relatively simple and straightforward model that does allow you some realistic tweaks of assumptions: the Financial Mentor Ultimate Retirement Calculator.

The Financial Mentor Ultimate Retirement Calculator

Financial guru Todd Tresidder created the Ultimate Financial Calculator (https://www.financialmentor.com/calculator/best-retirement-calculator) with the idea of combining some additional functionality and realism with simplicity and usability. The Ultimate Retirement Calculator does all the usual forecasting of retirement savings needs, accounting for longevity, return rates, and even adding a cost-of-living adjustment.

Beyond that, however, it allows you to plan a modern retirement with phased income, part-time business income, real estate income, inheritances, and other factors in a real retirement. You can add multiple income streams, specify their duration and growth, or plan the sale of a home or business. Scenario planning is easy, and there are tools to help you through it.

Figure 8.1 shows the input page.

Once the inputs are complete, you can hit the "Calculate" button to arrive at the results (see figure 8.2).

You can see the lump sum required and an estimate of what you need to save to get there, which should be familiar from the annuity math model. A supplemental report details out annual activity in your retirement.

This model is simple and easy to use yet has enough sophistication to approach reality. Like the first two models, it's a good way to get a handle on your savings needs for retirement.

> The three models offered here to estimate your retirement savings needs are simpler than many you'll find online. But they will get you pretty close, with straightforward answers and minimal effort.
>
> They'll give a good idea where you are and where you need to go.

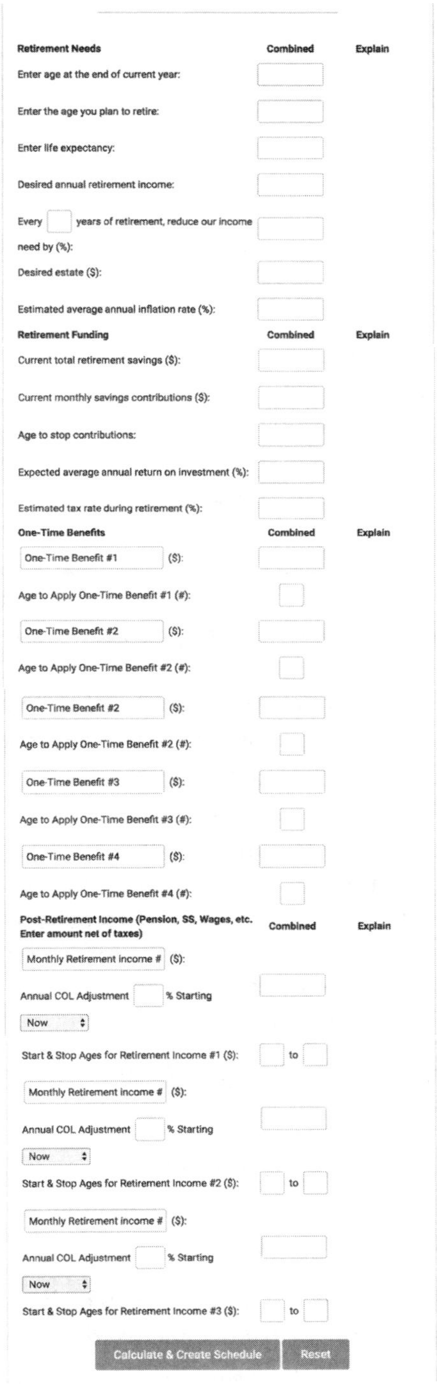

Retirement Needs	Combined	Explain
Enter age at the end of current year:		
Enter the age you plan to retire:		
Enter life expectancy:		
Desired annual retirement income:		
Every [ ] years of retirement, reduce our income need by (%):		
Desired estate ($):		
Estimated average annual inflation rate (%):		
Retirement Funding	**Combined**	**Explain**
Current total retirement savings ($):		
Current monthly savings contributions ($):		
Age to stop contributions:		
Expected average annual return on investment (%):		
Estimated tax rate during retirement (%):		
One-Time Benefits	**Combined**	**Explain**
One-Time Benefit #1 ($):		
Age to Apply One-Time Benefit #1 (#):		
One-Time Benefit #2 ($):		
Age to Apply One-Time Benefit #2 (#):		
One-Time Benefit #2 ($):		
Age to Apply One-Time Benefit #2 (#):		
One-Time Benefit #3 ($):		
Age to Apply One-Time Benefit #3 (#):		
One-Time Benefit #4 ($):		
Age to Apply One-Time Benefit #4 (#):		
Post-Retirement Income (Pension, SS, Wages, etc. Enter amount net of taxes)	**Combined**	**Explain**
Monthly Retirement income # ($):		
Annual COL Adjustment [ ] % Starting Now		
Start & Stop Ages for Retirement Income #1 ($):	[ ] to [ ]	
Monthly Retirement income # ($):		
Annual COL Adjustment [ ] % Starting Now		
Start & Stop Ages for Retirement Income #2 ($):	[ ] to [ ]	
Monthly Retirement income # ($):		
Annual COL Adjustment [ ] % Starting Now		
Start & Stop Ages for Retirement Income #3 ($):	[ ] to [ ]	

Calculate & Create Schedule | Reset

Figure 8.1. Ultimate Retirement Calculator Input

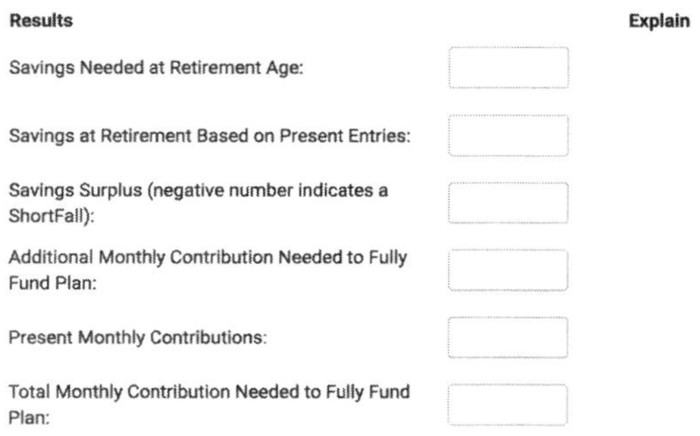

Results | **Explain**

Savings Needed at Retirement Age:

Savings at Retirement Based on Present Entries:

Savings Surplus (negative number indicates a ShortFall):

Additional Monthly Contribution Needed to Fully Fund Plan:

Present Monthly Contributions:

Total Monthly Contribution Needed to Fully Fund Plan:

Figure 8.2. Ultimate Retirement Calculator Results

Where We Go from Here

This chapter concludes part 1, which is all about understanding what you have and what you need to provide a secure, "rock-solid" retirement.

Several times throughout this narrative, I have brought up the concept of annuities (annuity *products*) as a way to expand beyond Social Security to provide a guaranteed, failsafe retirement income stream for life.

The bottom line is pretty simple: You need savings to make up for the gap between Social Security and your actual retirement needs. Annuities present an opportunity to convert *some* of those savings into a failsafe Social Security–like income stream, thus expanding your income security for life.

Part 2 describes annuity "products" in detail:

- Chapter 9 gives an overview of all types of annuities and how they work.
- Chapter 10 explains fixed annuities.
- Chapter 11 covers fixed indexed annuities.
- Chapter 12 covers variable annuities.
- Chapter 13 explores income riders, which can help guarantee returns on variable and some fixed indexed annuities.
- Chapter 14 reviews how annuities fit into your overall retirement plan.

By the Numbers

- **4.** The percentage you can withdraw every year from your retirement savings with a very low probability of running out of cash, assuming you follow simple rules
- **25.** The number multiplied by your annual income needs from savings used to estimate a lump sum required on Retirement Day One using the 4 percent rule
- **3 to 5.5.** The traditional percent range of adjustments of the 4 percent rule given certain assumptions and flexibilities in how you take your withdrawals (Recent low return rates suggest using even a lower withdrawal assumption.)
- **17.3.** The multiple of your annual income needs to arrive at a lump sum required on Retirement Day One, assuming 4 percent constant investment returns and even withdrawals using distribution annuity math
- **19.6.** What the multiple above rises to if your investment returns drop from 4 percent to 3 percent

PART 2

MONEY FOR LIFE

Using Annuities to Secure Your Retirement

The Income Revolution is divided into two parts. Part 1, "Retirement Crisis" (which you just finished if you're reading sequentially), gives an overview of today's retirement planning challenges and what to think about as you prepare your own retirement plan.

Along the way, part 1 shows how annuities can help bridge the retirement income gap between Social Security, (disappearing) pensions, and what you truly need for a comfortable, "rock-solid" retirement.

Sure, at the simplest level, you simply need money—savings—to bridge the gap. I showed how you could target, accumulate, and convert savings into a monthly or yearly income stream using simple annuity math or even the simpler but somewhat outdated "4 percent rule." Yes, you can do this yourself.

You sensed a "but" coming, and here it is: Sure, with the right discipline, a clear view of the future, and a degree of good fortune, you can do this yourself. *But* there are no guarantees. What if you live 20 years longer than you plan for with your savings? What if the markets don't perform as you expect, particularly in the first few years of retirement? What if you don't have the discipline to manage your withdrawals according to plan?

Wouldn't it be nice if you could buy insurance to cover these risks just like you can cover your life, home, or car? Well, it turns out you can—in the form of annuities. Annuities, in essence, are a form of insurance against outliving your money.

Such insurance helps guarantee that those regular checks arrive during retirement just like during your working years. Through *all* of your retirement. *Nothing to worry about.* If you're particularly risk adverse, you can get the same check for life. But, as we'll see, there are ways to participate in asset growth too (*growing* that check), while getting some or all of the guarantees offered by an annuity.

Now we reach part 2, in which I'll lay out and describe the world of annuities—what they are, how they work, how they can be customized to meet your needs, what they cost, how they fit into your retirement plan, and how to buy them.

The goal is not to make you an "expert" or to prepare you for an insurance license exam to sell annuities. As we'll see, some annuities can be complex and vary greatly between one offering and the next. The differences can be subtle. Even the *terminology* differs from one insurance company to the next and from one *agent* to the next. Unlike many other investment and financial products like stocks, CDs, or mutual funds, most annuities do not lend themselves to the do-it-yourselfer.

Hence the idea of part 2 (really the entire book) is to present the basics of annuities—what they do and how they work—so that you can "be smart" when you talk to a professional. You'll be smart enough to follow the discussion and to ask the right questions. You'll be smart enough to figure out what kind of annuity—and what kinds of options (called "riders")—best serve your needs.

Part 2 gives an overview of annuities and then details particular types of annuities. You won't know about all the options or exactly what annuity to buy. But if you can understand the choices and how they fit your retirement plan, I've done my job.

CHAPTER 9

ANNUITIES

An Old Idea with Modern Advantages

What *Is* an Annuity, Anyhow?

An annuity is a contractual agreement between a buyer (owner) and an insurance company (seller). Annuities are used to save for retirement and/or to convert accumulated wealth into a stream of income immediately or sometime in the future.

To generate an income stream, an individual purchases an annuity and the insurance company makes a promise to make regular payments (income) that begin on a specific future date—or, in the case of "immediate" annuities, immediately. Annuities can be purchased by anyone, and they are primarily used by people who wish to generate a stream of income during retirement. That said, many annuities are purchased for wealth accumulation purposes as well.

An annuity is a product. And like most products, it has a core benefit—to protect and enhance your retirement income—in return for a charge or a cost. Like most products, there are many different kinds of annuities you can buy to serve specific needs, concerns, and interests in retirement. And there are a lot of features and options you can add onto the annuity to "customize" it to your own situation—again for a cost, usually a modest one. I'll cover some of those add-on features, called "riders," later in this chapter.

> An annuity is a contractual agreement between a buyer and an insurance company.
>
> Annuities are used to save for retirement and/or to convert accumulated wealth into an income stream immediately or sometime in the future.
>
> Annuities are a form of insurance against outliving your money.

Not a New Idea...

Annuities may sound like some newfangled contraption conceived under the banner of "financial engineering" in the halls of an Ivy League business school in the heady days before the 2008–9 financial crisis.

Nothing could be further from the truth.

In fact, the concept of annuities dates back to the Roman Empire, when retired soldiers received what amounts to an annuity—an income stream—as compensation for military service. During the Middle Ages, feudal kings used annuities to cover the cost of war.

Annuities first came to America in the mid-1700s, when pools funded by parishioner contributions were used to provide income for retired church pastors in Pennsylvania. Ben Franklin, ever concerned about civic welfare, gave annuities to the cities of Boston and Philadelphia in his will—the last of which was just cashed out for its lump sum value in 1990!

Today's modern annuity isn't funded by kings, military leaders, parishioners, or founding fathers. The concept carries over from those days, but today's annuity is typically funded by you and created, packaged, and sold by an insurance company. It is a financial agreement between the insurance company and the customer, usually sold through a trained and licensed agent representing the insurance company. Modern annuities have been routinely sold since the early 20th century.

A Bet Against Your Life

"An insurance company?" you might quip. "Why would something you pay for, and expect a return from, be funded by an insurance company? I thought insurance companies existed to take your money and pay you nothing! Here, with the annuity, they are contracting to pay you *something*. Isn't that an *investment* rather than an insurance policy?"

You're on the right track. Insurance companies take premiums in the hope of paying you (or the collective "you"—all policy holders) something a little less than the premiums paid in and what they are able to earn by investing those premium dollars. That's largely how they make a profit.

When an insurance company sells you a life insurance policy, they collect a premium in the hopes that you won't die during the coverage period, thus saving them from ever paying a death benefit.

When an insurance company sells you an annuity, guaranteeing payment of an income stream for a period of years or life, they are betting that you will die sooner than the end of the annuity (and as we'll see, "period-certain" riders help the annuity owners lessen that gamble). It's the same idea, just the opposite bet. Actuaries at the insurance company look at average life expectancies and price for what *is likely* to happen. They stand to benefit if you kick the bucket sooner than you're supposed to.

If you buy an annuity, does that mean you have to keep your eyes peeled for sunglasses-wearing thugs hired by insurance companies tasked to rub you out immediately? Heck no! Their bases are covered by other annuity holders in the pool: If you don't die when you're "supposed to," someone else will.

No Free Lunch: How the Insurance Company Makes Money

Especially when you buy a complex product, it's a good idea to understand how the seller makes its money. If you understand the motives, you'll understand the product better, and you're more likely to get what you pay for.

When an insurance company sells you an annuity, they are taking on risk, and they charge a premium for that risk—just as with any insurance policy or product. Insurance companies assume risk when they guarantee your future payments. Those risks include such things as interest rate risk, market risk, and the risk of you living longer than your life expectancy.

In return for assuming such risks, the insurer sells you a contract and collects a premium. Depending on the type of annuity and the contract, they may make money from

- *Upfront and ongoing fees.* These can include sales, administrative, and investment management fees.
- *Surrender fees.* These are charges for terminating the contract early, which can be quite steep and punitive; insurance companies want to hold onto your money as long as possible.
- *Early death or termination.* Insurance companies make money on "life annuities" if you die sooner than the actuarial expectation.
- *"Float."* This is attained by profitably investing all those dollars collected for all those years before they have to pay them out. Just ask Warren Buffett how much money can be made on insurance "float"!

When an insurance company sells you an annuity, they are taking on a risk.

The "risk" is that your paid-in principal will lose value and that you'll outlive your expected lifespan.

Part of your up-front payment into an annuity is a "premium" to take on this risk.

The "Sucker Factor" and How It Works *for* You

A sucker factor working *for* you? Never thought you'd hear those words together. What gives?

Suppose you bought an annuity for $50,000 in the early years of annuities. Then you got hit and killed by a streetcar on the way home. What happened to the $50,000? The insurance company kept it! Never had to make out a single check to you. Sucker!

Nowadays, there are many people in a given annuity pool, and a few of them will die early. What happens? Yes, the insurance company keeps those premiums too, but typically at least some portion of that excess cash is used to enhance contracted annuity payments for those who survive. You get more out of the bad fortune of others; that's a good thing (except for the few unfortunates).

And to minimize the risk of this "sucker factor," which naturally kept many from buying annuities, insurance companies started offering guarantees in the form of survivorship payments (you can designate a survivor to receive you payments if you die) and "period-certain" riders, which oblige the insurer to pay a lump sum upon death for up to 20 years after the annuity purchase.

These features guarantee you won't lose everything if you get hit by that streetcar! Of course, both of these protections cost a bit more (in the form of lowered payouts), and you should still look both ways before crossing the street.

What Annuities Do for You

Admittedly I'm jumping the gun here a bit, describing the value provided by annuities before I've described their many forms and how they work. But let me give this to you as a preamble: You'll see how these benefits and advantages—especially as compared to ordinary investments—come about as you read on.

- *Predictability.* As we saw in chapters 6 and 7, markets can be quite volatile and can really take apart your best intentions, especially when losses happen in the early stages of retirement. Substantial losses at retirement age can devastate a nest egg with no time to recover, but annuities can guarantee fixed payments no matter what the market does. The insurance company assumes the risk; you sleep at night.
- *Life payment.* Annuities are unique in that they are the only financial product that can provide a guaranteed payout for as long as you live. No other financial product—CDs, bonds, mutual funds, and so on—can do that.

- *No contribution limits.* Most retirement savings vehicles—401(k)s, IRAs, and so on—have annual contribution limits that can be quite restrictive if you're trying to play catch-up. Annuities have a minimum, usually $1,000, but for most of us, practically no maximum (most max out at $1 million, and you can exceed this amount by buying more than one annuity).
- *Tax deferral.* No contribution limits, but tax deferral anyhow. Sweet! Annuity earnings accumulate tax-deferred. And when your payout phase begins, you pay taxes only on the earnings, while some of your payment will be nontaxable return of principal. Advantage: annuities.
- *Some liquidity.* Most think that once you commit funds to an annuity, you're committed for life, and those funds will be tied up and unable to meet unanticipated needs. But many annuities have a penalty-free withdrawal provision, usually up to 10 percent per year. There are other options such as long-term care or medical riders that can also release funds early. Typically once the surrender period has expired—usually 5 to 10 years—you'll have access to your money, penalty free.
- *Safety.* Markets are volatile, and studies have shown that you will become a less-successful investor as you get older. Fixed and fixed indexed annuities are not a *security* and thus are not afforded the protections of deposit insurance or Securities and Exchange Commission scrutiny; they are regulated by the state insurance departments. Variable annuities are regulated by the state insurance departments and the SEC. All annuities are *contracts,* and many are offered by some of the safest and long-lived companies in the world. I'll discuss some of the implications of this difference and how to evaluate insurance company safety.

Annuity advantages include predictable life income, tax deferral, unlimited contributions, and safety.

Never Considered an Annuity? You're Not Alone

I suspect that many of you reading this book don't own annuities. You've heard something about them but have stuck to your guns with your investments and traditional employer and individual retirement plans. You do it yourself or may have a traditional financial planner, registered investment advisor, or broker working with you and for you.

This is the typical approach. And many like you, as a consequence, haven't heard much about annuities.

Are they too complex? Not really. Are they just not for you? No, they are—there's a good chance they could work very well for you. So why don't you hear much from your traditional investment advisors about annuities?

There are two reasons.

First, if an advisor points you to annuities, your money will be committed to that product, and your advisor won't make any more money managing your money.

Second, most annuities are sold through the insurance industry and require insurance licensing—not investment licensing—to sell! (An exception is variable annuities, which are both investment and insurance, require a registered investment advisor [RIA] designation, a Series 6 or 7 securities license, *and* an insurance license to sell.)

Adding to the annuity blind spot is the fact that fee-only financial planners can't take a commission for selling annuities and thus aren't motivated at all, particularly since the investment value under their prerogative would go away.

Here's the upshot: The reason many haven't considered annuities lies not in what they are but in who's selling them! A good financial advisor looking out for your interests should be able and willing to answer your questions and point you in the right direction (to a licensed agent if they aren't licensed themselves).

And beware—the blind spots work the other way too—if you go to an insurance-licensed annuity specialist, you may not get the unbiased view of your whole financial picture, including your other retirement investments.

I hope this channel conflict disappears someday. In the meantime, know who sells what, get help with the big picture, and don't be afraid to talk to an annuity specialist. Especially after reading this book, you'll be well prepared for the conversation!

Many annuities are sold through insurance channels, not investment channels. That may be why you haven't heard much about them or considered them until now.

What Kinds of Annuities Can I Buy?

As described previously, annuities are contracts, and fixed and fixed indexed annuities are not securities. As such, they don't have any preordained structure or definition laid out by securities regulators. They can be custom designed and crafted to meet any given market need.

That is both an advantage and a disadvantage. It's an advantage because you can really tailor an annuity to your needs. If you have 15 years to retirement, a moderate risk tolerance, a spouse, possible health issues, and expect to inherit money at or about the time of retirement, you can find and build out an annuity with moderate growth participation and delay payments until some years after retirement.

The custom nature of annuities also makes them harder to understand—there are very few "boilerplate" annuity standards—and even the terminology varies from one carrier to the next!

That said, annuities can be classified into basic types for the sake of discussion and planning. The bells and whistles might vary, but nearly all annuities fit into certain well-established categories.

First, "Accumulation" and "Distribution"

Before presenting the classification, it will help to note that most annuities have an *accumulation* (pay-in and growth) period and a *distribution* (payout) period. The exception is "immediate" annuities (described shortly), which by definition have no accumulation period.

During the accumulation period, you build value into the annuity. You pay in funds of your own, and depending on the type of annuity, the asset value may also grow, either by crediting interest or by participating in the investment markets. Specific accumulation vehicles include

- *Lump sum.* This is a single payment that can be before, at, or during retirement.
- *Regular contributions.* These are like savings, usually before retirement.
- *Interest and investment gains.* These are for annuities designed to pay out several years down the road. Depending on the type, they will accumulate interest, investment gains, or both.
- *A combination of the above three.*

During the distribution period, usually after retirement, the annuity pays out its value. This can be done in one of many ways:

- *Lump sum.* This is a single payment of all accumulated value.
- *"Annuitizing."* This option irrevocably converts the annuity into a constant payment stream.
- *Something else.* This can be determined by an optional income rider or some other mechanism.
- *A combination of the above three.*

You have choices about when and how to accumulate and distribute, depending on your risk tolerance, timing before retirement, and overall objectives.

> There are many ways that annuities can accumulate and distribute wealth.

Now, let's move on to the specific classification used by many industry professionals and annuity holders.

Premium Payment Schedule

"Payment schedule" refers to how and when you pay into the annuity. The choices are

- *Single payment.* This is the lump sum paid up front—either right when you expect to receive distributions (immediate) or at a certain time period before you wish to receive distributions (deferred).
- *Flexible payment.* You may choose to pay over time, a certain amount per month or year or whenever you can. This can be additional to a lump sum. This option typically occurs only with deferred annuities—that is, annuities that pay out several years down the road.

Payout Timing

Payout timing refers to how and when you're paid out. The two choices—which I've already alluded to—are

- *Immediate.* You can buy an annuity and convert it into an income stream right away. Many do this when they reach retirement age or want to lock in an income stream for life later on in retirement. The payout method is *annuitization* into a constant payment stream.
- *Deferred.* Here, you buy an annuity and let it grow for a while before starting a payout. The annuity has a growth element and can be paid out in a lump sum, by annuitizing, or by some other contractual approach, like an income rider. As we'll see shortly, most annuity sales are of the deferred variety.

Annuity Type

Here is where most of you who have read about or owned annuities find familiar ground. There are three major types of annuities corresponding to different levels of investment exposure and participation in growth—from no to a limited tracking to full participation in investment growth.

- *Fixed annuities.* These are just as the term says—the interest credited is fixed. Fixed deferred annuities receive a fixed interest rate, which may be adjusted or *reset* by contract after a given number of years. There is no investment risk in fixed annuities. Your returns are fixed and governed by contract; the insurance company assumes the risk.

- *Fixed indexed annuities.* These are an evolution of fixed annuities and have a feature that allows limited tracking of the markets without full participation in the markets or market risk. They are constructed to eliminate downside market risk. You aren't invested directly in the markets and thus don't get all the gains in an expanding market, but you can avoid losses, and your annuity value can grow over time. Again, the insurance company assumes the downside risk but offers you a limited potential for upside gain.
- *Variable annuities.* Think of these as investment vehicles with annuity features built in. Through investment vehicles chosen by the annuity owner, these annuities accumulate or lose value according to market performance. In a sense, they are mutual funds with tax benefits and the benefits of annuitization and riders to govern and extend payouts. Prior to annuitization—that is, in the accumulation phase—they are *not* guaranteed by the insurance company. Currently they are the largest-selling annuity segment but are declining in popularity as fixed indexed annuities (FIAs) become more popular with their risk-minimizing provisions.

These annuity types are pervasive through the discussion of annuities; you can pick one from Column A, one from Column B, and one from Column C to describe almost any annuity. A "single premium immediate fixed annuity" can be distinguished from a "flexible premium deferred fixed indexed annuity," although you won't always hear these exact terms.

It should be noted that because of their characteristics, almost all variable and fixed indexed annuities are deferred—that is, they have a definite nonzero accumulation period.

The "type" classification provides the framework for the next three chapters as I discuss each type in detail.

Annuities can generally be classified by type and timing of pay-in and payout.

Pay-in timing can be *single* or *flexible*—that is, over time.

Payout timing can be *immediate* or *deferred*.

Key types include *fixed*, *fixed indexed*, and *variable*.

What Kinds of Annuities Do Other People Buy?

By nature, we humans love to compare!

When making a complex decision like buying annuities, it often helps to look at what others around us are doing. It helps to validate, and it also helps to identify where to spend our time. Which types of annuities sell the most? Which types are *growing* the most?

To help answer these questions, I'll share data prepared at the end of 2015 by the Life Insurance Management Research Association (LIMRA), an excellent research and reference source for the industry (see table 9.1). These stats show amounts and year-over-year growth for key annuity types.

TABLE 9.1. Annual Sales by Annuity Type

Annuity Type	2015 Sales ($ Billions)	Percent of Total	Percent Change Versus 2014
Fixed immediate	2.3	1.0%	–6
Fixed deferred	31.9	13.5	9
Fixed indexed	54.5	23.0	13
Variable	133.0	56.2	–5
Other	15.0	6.3	1
Total	236.7	100	0

Source: LIMRA Secure Retirement Institute, US Individual Annuity Sales Survey, 2015, Q4

As you can see, with 64 years of sales history, variable annuities are still the winners, accounting for more than half of wannuity sales. But variable annuity sales are declining as fixed indexed annuities, which have been sold for about 21 years, with their loss protection characteristics, gain in popularity.

While variable annuities are still most popular, fixed indexed annuities are gaining ground rapidly.

I *Know* Investing Is Risky: What Are the Risks of Annuities?

Most annuities are designed with one idea in mind—to provide a steady and reliable cash flow now or sometime in the future that you can count on. That makes them inherently less risky than traditional investments, which come with no guarantees at all.

That said, there are risks inherent in some or all annuities:

- *Solvency risks—for all annuities.* Annuities do not have "institutional" protections such as FDIC or SIPC like their bank deposit and securities brethren. Rather, they are guaranteed only by the full faith and credit of the insurance company that sells them. If that company ceases to exist, your annuity might be in jeopardy. There are varying state-level guarantees (more below).
- *Investment risks—for variable annuities only.* Because the value of variable annuity is tied to an investment portfolio, there is risk inherent in market performance and your choice of investments for that portfolio.

How Annuities Stack Up Against Other Types of Investments

You may see a "risk pyramid" like the one in figure 9.1 when you talk with a financial or annuity professional. The pyramid outlines the risks of different kinds of annuities relative to other kinds of investments. You can see how annuities effectively transfer investment risk to the insurance company, giving you peace of mind now and in the future.

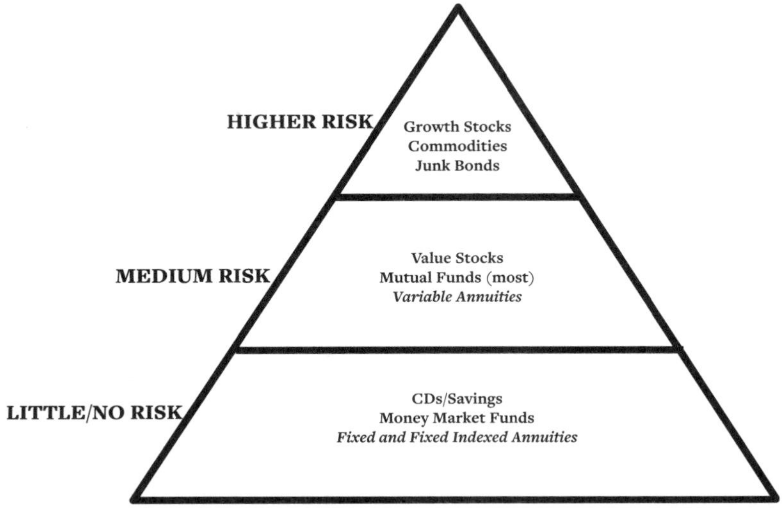

Figure 9.1. Investment and Annuity Risk Pyramid

> Most types of annuities are safer than most types of investments.

How Annuities Are Regulated and Protected

This section elaborates on the "solvency risk" mentioned previously and discusses how to protect against that risk.

When you purchase an annuity, the guaranteed elements of the annuity are backed by the financial strength and claims-paying ability of the issuing insurer. Annuities are regulated by each individual state's Department of Insurance. Annuities aren't guaranteed by the FDIC or any other federal government agency, but there are strict capital and reserve requirements that necessitate insurance companies to hold one dollar in reserve for every dollar in benefits owed. Annuity companies typically invest in very conservative financial instruments like high-quality corporate and US government bonds.

In practice, insurance company defaults are very rare; in 20 years of history with the recently popular fixed indexed annuities, there have been none. Zero. I'll also note that even in bankruptcy, a total loss of annuity value is unlikely because the claims of annuity creditors would likely take priority over many other claims against the company.

Making the Grade: The Insurance Company Rating System

Are you just a bit frightened at the thought of having to assess an insurance company's financial strength and soundness before "taking the plunge" into buying an annuity? Heck, you have enough trouble assessing your own financial soundness from time to time, right?

Fortunately, much of the homework has been done for you. There are no fewer than four separate ratings agencies—A. M. Best, Moody's, Standard & Poors, and Fitch—that evaluate nearly all annuity providers and provide handy letter grades denoting their strength, risk management, and ability to meet their future financial obligations, including annuity payments. A. M. Best specializes in the insurance industry, while the other three firms rate insurance companies as part of a larger securities analysis business.

Appendix A of this book details the rating "grades," top to bottom, given by the ratings agencies. Most annuity buyers should stay in the top two or three ratings brackets, although naturally the top products for safety may be more conservative by paying out a bit less. Here are the "top" grades for the four agencies:

- A. M. Best:
    - *A++, A+.* Superior—able to meet insurance obligations
    - *A, A–.* Excellent—able to meet insurance obligations
    - *B++, B+.* Good—able to meet insurance obligations
- Moody's:
    - *AAA.* Extremely strong—market conditions are unlikely to affect a fundamentally strong position
    - *AA.* Very strong—high-grade company with marginally larger long-term risks
    - *A.* Strong—financially secure but signs of long-term susceptibility
    - *Baa.* Adequate—lacking in certain protective elements over the long term

- Standard & Poors:
  - *AAA*. Extremely strong—very unlikely to be affected by adverse economic conditions
  - *AA*. Very strong—unlikely to be affected by adverse economic conditions
  - *A*. Strong—marginally more likely to be affected by adverse economic conditions
  - *BBB*. Good—may be affected by adverse business conditions
- Fitch:
  - *AAA*. Exceptionally strong—very unlikely to be affected by adverse economic conditions
  - *AA*. Very strong—not significantly vulnerable to adverse economic conditions
  - *A*. Strong—low expectation for interruption of payments
  - *BBB*. Good—may be affected by adverse economic conditions

It's good practice to engage with companies that have top ratings, although many companies in the middle ranges have been paying effectively for years.

State Guarantee Protection Limits

Beyond the "full faith and credit" of insurance companies as evaluated by the ratings agencies, state life and health insurance guaranty associations—known as state guaranty associations—provide a safety net for their state's policyholders, ensuring that they continue to receive coverage even if their insurer is declared insolvent.

Once again, annuities are not federally regulated or insured (no FDIC), but each insurance company is licensed and regulated in states in which it conducts business. Each state covers policies up to a certain amount should the company go bankrupt through the state guaranty associations. Coverages typically vary around $100,000 per policy for the typical annuity but can range up to $300,000. This is why it's a good idea, if you have a lot of cash to buy annuities, to spread it among several contracts.

More information about specific coverages by state can be found in Appendix C of this book, and more info about state guaranty associations in general can be found at the National Organization of Life & Health Guaranty Associations website at https://www.nolhga.com.

> Annuities are regulated at the state level.
>
> Annuities aren't guaranteed by the federal government or backed by any national public resource or fund.
>
> Annuities are backed by the strength of the issuing insurance company and may have some backing at the state level.

Any Color but Black: The Many Ways Annuities Can Be Customized

You buy a car. It comes in several base models typically designed to satisfy the tastes, interests, and needs of different customers. You pick out a model. But are you done yet? In a word, no: There are many more options available, most of which you have to pay for, that "soup up" a car to fit your individual needs and tastes—anything from paint colors to special wheels to sunroofs to extended warranties.

It is much the same with annuities. You choose a base model—anything from a simple fixed immediate to a fixed indexed annuity to a more complex variable annuity—suited to what you're trying to accomplish. Then you can add options to tailor them to your needs, your risk profile, your medical conditions, and your desire to pass money on to your heirs. Such options are called *riders*.

For the sake of discussion, I'll divide riders into two groups: simple and complex. "Simple" riders are just that: short, usually inexpensive enhancements generally available on all types of annuities to guarantee payouts or set up earlier or larger payouts for certain events or situations. "Complex" riders are typically designed for variable and some fixed indexed annuities to enhance the payouts in case of market failure and decline in underlying annuity value.

I will go over the available riders in the following sections.

A Short Menu of Simple Riders

- *Period certain, or guaranteed payback riders.* These riders guard against "sucker factor" failure—the loss of all annuity principal if you die early—by making payments "certain" for a number of years (usually 10, 15, or 20) to a beneficiary or as a lump sum.
- *Refund rider.* A more limited version of the period certain rider, this guarantees that your heirs will receive the residual value of the annuity either as a lump sum or in installments. It is typically used for fixed immediate annuities.
- *Cost of living or inflation adjusted rider.* To protect against inflation, this rider can be set for fixed percentage or tied to the consumer price index like Social Security to increase annuity benefits over time.
- *Disability, unemployment, or terminal illness riders.* Typically available for deferred annuities, these riders allow you to tap into principal without penalty in the case of terminal illness, disability, or unemployment.
- *Nursing home/long-term care rider.* Upon diagnosed need for long-term care, this rider allows for a lump sum or increased payout to cover the additional cost of nursing homes, assisted living, or in-home care.
- *Commuted payout rider.* For immediate annuities, this rider allows you to withdraw a lump sum without penalty should the need arise—with a maximum percentage of the premium paid. It essentially guarantees access to your money committed for as much as a lifetime by the annuity.
- *Impaired risk rider.* This rider allows for a boost in annuity payments upon diagnosis of a major disease or illness during the payout period.

Each rider typically adds somewhere between 0 and 1.0 percent to the cost of the annuity or may affect the amount of your payouts once you enter the distribution phase. (I include "zero" because many annuity contracts include the rider[s] at no extra charge.) The list of riders—and their variations—is extensive. All provide value; it's just a matter of personal preference and the need to choose which is best for you.

Complex "Income" Riders

As I've noted, variable annuities come with some risk of loss of value and thus the ability to pay a "guaranteed" income stream when you need it. To mitigate that risk, the insurance industry came up with a series of riders to "guarantee" an income or withdrawal stream based on a valuation base and formula different from the annuity's actual value. Thus you can lose value on the annuity but still preserve your income stream if you buy one of these riders:

- guaranteed lifetime withdrawal benefit (GMLB) rider
- guaranteed minimum accumulation benefit (GMAB) rider
- guaranteed minimum income benefit (GMIB) rider
- guaranteed minimum withdrawal benefit (GMWB) rider

The mechanics of these riders, and the choices among them, are complex enough to warrant a separate chapter, so I'll cover them in chapter 13.

> Simple and complex riders can be used to customize an annuity to your needs and risk tolerance.

And What Does All This Cost?

Aside from complexity, the major downside of some annuities can be summed up in one word: fees. Fees and costs usually come in three doses:

- *Commissions.* Commissions are paid to sales agents by the insurance company, not by you directly, and not as a deduction against the value of your annuity.

- *Surrender charges.* If you withdraw funds beyond prescribed limits sooner than the contract allows, you will be hit with often substantial surrender charges, which are deducted from the withdrawal. When shopping for an annuity, you should match the surrender period to the length of time you think you can avoid tapping into this asset.

- *Other fees.* Typically relegated to variable annuities only, there are other fees akin to investment management fees for mutual funds: administrative fees, fees for making investment changes, and so forth.
- *Riders.* The wide assortment of riders used to customize annuities all come with their own costs, usually deducted from the principal value of the annuity.

Some of these fees occur only one time, usually up front, in the annuity contract life. Some, like investment management fees, can be ongoing. All fees and costs should be spelled out in the annuity contract, which you should read carefully.

Commissions and Fees

Quite rightly, by now you're probably curious about just how much these fees and commissions can cost. Higher commissions mean two things: (1) the insurance company needs to recover that cost and will set up mechanisms elsewhere to do so and (2) your agent will have more incentive to sell that product. Buyer beware—it is best to find an agent representing many insurance/annuity lines (to get choices) and who has your best interests in mind.

Waving the White Flag: Surrender Charges

Holding and investing your money is part of how insurance companies make money selling annuities. So they have a reason to levy surrender charges to annuity buyers who withdraw too much from the annuity during the first few years of the contract.

Generally speaking, most annuity contracts allow a 10 percent annual withdrawal—but if an unexpected need requires you to withdraw more than 10 percent, you'll face a surrender charge on that amount. Surrender periods typically range from 3 to 10 years or more. The charges are levied as a percentage and typically vary from 2 to 7 to sometimes 10 percent or more, normally declining in tiers as you get farther out (7 percent in the first three years, 5 percent in the next two, 2 percent in the last two years of a 7-year surrender period is typical).

The surrender charge is part of the value proposition of the annuity. Generally shorter surrender periods and lower charges are better, but make sure you aren't losing value somewhere else. That said, a longer surrender period offers the insurance company more opportunity to earn income, so you should get better terms overall. If you can handle a longer surrender period, it might be worth it. Of course, try to set up your financial plan so you won't have to rely on a surrendered annuity.

"The Feeling Is Mutual" May Cost More than You Think

Okay, with all the commissions, fees, surrender, and other charges you've read about and heard about, you're probably thinking, "Most mutual funds charge 1 percent or less in fees these days. I could save myself a whole bunch of money by simply investing in a mutual fund and managing my withdrawals myself using the 4 percent rule or some such."

Wrong.

Yes, while the advertised average mutual fund "expense ratio" is about 0.90 percent these days—better than the 1.5 percent of days past—there are many hidden costs to owning mutual funds most investors don't even see, let alone know about.

Financial advisor Ty Bernicke lists the true and often hidden costs of owning a mutual fund in an April 2011 *Forbes* magazine article. He notes that in addition to the well-publicized expense ratio—which covers basic management, marketing, and distribution costs for the fund—at least five other costs get swept under the carpet:

- *Transaction costs.* Fees and commissions for making trades are charged to the fund, just like they would be if you traded stocks or bonds individually. Less obvious are the "spread" between bid and offer prices for stocks and bonds bought or sold by the fund and price concessions for buying or selling large blocks of securities. These charges come out the funds balance ("net asset value") and are mostly transparent to investors. One study put the price tag at 1.44 percent for the average equity fund.
- *"Cash drag."* Funds must keep a certain amount of cash on hand to handle expenses and redemptions. As this cash earns little to no return, it reduces fund performance compared to the averages and has no comparable equivalent in the annuity space. Another study put this cost at 0.83 percent for large stock funds.

- *"Soft dollar" cost.* An adjunct to transaction costs, brokers and professional advisory firms offering investment research advice also charge higher commissions and fees. These "soft" costs may be as much as 40 percent of all fund trading costs.
- *Advisory fees.* On top of the fees charged to the fund balance, as an individual you may pay another fee to a financial advisor to help choose and manage your funds and other investments. Typical fees are 1 percent annually.
- *Taxes.* In a taxable account, taxes will be assessed on capital gains often imbedded in the asset value before the individual buys the fund, leaving the individual investor with a tax bill when these gains are realized. Morningstar estimates the average tax cost for imbedded gains at 1 to 1.2 percent per year.

Here's the upshot: Even leaving the tax costs out, the true percentage cost for owning a mutual fund may be as high as 4 to 5 percent (0.90 percent + 1.44 percent + 0.83 percent + 1.00 percent) *annually.*

While commissions are not directly deducted from your contract, they are an expense that the company pays in most annuity sales, which is spread over all annuity contracts as a cost of doing business. There can be ongoing fees for some annuities (mostly variable), but keep in mind that most annuity costs are in the same ballpark from one company to the next and *only occur once,* not annually.

Comparing annuity fees and commissions with the total costs of owning a mutual fund, annuities aren't such a bad deal—assuming you don't surrender early.

Commissions, fees, and costs vary by type of annuity and are highest for variable annuities.

Many fees are one-time only and can compare quite favorably to comparable mutual fund investments.

Tax Stuff

Anyone thinking about annuities should make him or herself aware of the tax features and advantages (and one disadvantage) of annuities. The tax features can be significant and are summed up as follows:

- *Tax deferral.* Like IRAs, 401(k)s, and so on, earnings inside an annuity grow and compound tax-deferred—that is, no tax is owed until they are withdrawn, which is typically when you'll be in a lower tax bracket.
- *Unlimited contributions.* Unlike IRAs, 401(k)s, and so on, you can contribute any amount to an annuity. Win a million bucks in the lottery? Congratulations—you can dump it all into an annuity if you want.
- *Contributions can be in after tax (nonqualified) or pretax (qualified) dollars.* If you buy an annuity with after-tax dollars, you do not get to deduct contributions. But then the principal you receive later in the payout is thus nontaxable; tax has already been paid on it.
- *Payouts for nonqualified annuities aren't fully taxable.* When you receive an annuity payout, a portion of that payout is considered return of principal and is therefore excluded from taxation. The exact portion is determined by the exclusion ratio, which calculates how much of each payment is principal versus earnings. This "feature" reduces the tax impact of payments received in retirement.
- *Early withdrawals are subject to penalties.* Like IRAs, 401(k) s, and so on, early withdrawals of earnings (not principal) before age 59 ½ are subject to the 10 percent federal penalty for early withdrawal.
- *Required minimum distributions.* Like IRAs, 401(k)s, and so on, most annuities are subject to required minimum distributions (RMDs)—formulaic distributions that must be taken starting at age 70 ½. The exception to this are qualified longevity annuity contracts (QLACs). These contracts, recognized by the IRS in 2014, were designed as a late-life deferred annuity to guarantee against superlongevity, which defers the RMD age from 70 ½ to as late as 85.

- *No capital gains preference.* This is one of the few tax disadvantages of annuities, where capital gains accrued through variable annuities are taxed at ordinary, not capital-gains, rates, which could be as much as 19 percent higher (federal) for a high-earnings annuity holder. Note that this tax isn't owed until the earnings are paid out.
- *State premium taxes.* Be aware that there may be a state premium tax that varies from state to state—often paid when you surrender or annuitize an annuity. It typically ranges from 0.25 to 2.50 percent. Recently such taxes existed in only seven states and Puerto Rico. Before you buy, find out.

Remember, this is a summary. As with all tax matters, it's good form to consult with an expert.

Liability Protection

Annuities can provide a way to protect assets from creditors in certain states. The exemption ranges from a few hundred dollars in some states to an unlimited amount in others. In some states, all annuities are exempt, while in others, only annuities payable to one's spouse, children, or other dependents are exempt. Protection is defined by the state in which the annuity is created, not the state in which the buyer lives. Some foreign-sourced annuities, such as those sold in Switzerland, also provide protection if you live in a state that doesn't offer liability protection.

This feature can provide important protection for individuals involved in tort-vulnerable professions, such as medical professionals. Your annuity professional should know whether any annuity you're considering is protected.

> Annuities enjoy the advantages of tax deferral, and on a nonqualified annuity, you're only taxed on the income portion of a payout, not the principal if you buy it with after-tax dollars.
>
> Annuities are subject to most taxation rules applicable to retirement accounts.
>
> Annuities may afford some liability protection in some states.

The Best Way to Buy Annuities

Some annuities can be complicated and confusing to understand. (That's why you're reading this book!)

Using the services of an agency that has trained professionals to guide you through the process is preferable to trying to go it alone. An agent can help you compare the various types of annuities offered by different insurance companies and inform you on which contracts and riders are available in your state. They can show quotes outlining payouts specific to your set of criteria and desired options. With so many annuity products on the market being offered by a wide range of insurance companies, it may benefit you to work with an independent agent that represents more than just one insurance company.

Using an independent agent that has access to the annuity products offered by many different companies, and is experienced in all the complexities of annuities, can help ensure that you get the best annuity for your situation. Purchasing an annuity is a big financial decision, so you want to be sure that you are buying the right annuity appropriate for your objectives.

About the Rest of Part 2

This chapter gave you a midlevel overview of annuities—what they are; how they work; the different types, features, benefits, facts, and figures; and a few of the downsides.

The next three chapters (chapters 10, 11, and 12) dive in a little deeper into the detail of fixed, fixed index, and variable annuities, respectively. Chapter 13 paints a little more of the detail about income riders, a safety and security feature designed mainly for variable annuities. These chapters focus on the mechanics, examples, and where and how to use each annuity type and feature.

Chapter 14 sums up the planning and use of annuities as part of retirement, offers some important tips, explains how to buy annuities, and sums up the annuity conversation.

CHAPTER 10

FIXED ANNUITIES

The Simplest Choice

Your retirement party just ended.

The last of your coworkers heads out the door, saying "Congratulations!" just one final time. You absorbed the office clown's last tease about long days in a rocking chair on your porch. Your boss smiles and whispers something to your coworkers before they drive off. You gather your gifts, look around one more time, and head for the door yourself.

What an exhilarating feeling! Free at last. Free to read, plant roses, visit the grandkids, or hold court with your buddies at the nearby donut shop. Free to travel, hike, boat, knit, sew . . .

But your thoughts stop in their tracks. That paycheck everybody else has coming on the first of the month won't be coming your way. No more friendly direct deposit notices. You had a steady income stream. Counted on it—depended on it—for years. And now it's gone.

Filling the Gap

Many a retiree has gone through the euphoria of retirement only to descend to terra firma with a resounding thud when he or she realizes the impact of not having that regular paycheck.

Now, if you played your cards right, you have—or will soon receive—Social Security. You have some retirement savings. If you're smart, your home is paid off so you no longer *need* so much income. And if you're *really* lucky, you have a traditional private or public sector pension that fills the gap and has features to keep up with inflation. (If so, please stop reading here and hand the book to someone else!)

Most of us don't have such a stable income stream at our disposal. An income stream that is large enough and, more important, guaranteed to last as long as we will. A secure income stream that will also take care of a spouse.

Nope—most of us simply have Social Security and whatever savings we've managed to accumulate.

"What's wrong with that picture?" you might ask. Well, nothing, nothing at all if you have enough savings to last and to endure the ups and downs of the investment world. It's true that if you have enough savings (millions), you probably don't have much to worry about.

But again, back to the world of most mere mortals. We need some savings in retirement to handle unexpected expenses and to grow with inflation. But subjecting all of our savings to the whims of the markets, and subjecting ourselves to the danger of lasting 10 years longer than our money does, is hardly good medicine for any of us.

Wouldn't we all like to have one of those pensions? A steady, predicable, no fears, no worries, last-as-long-as-we-need income stream to carry us and our loved ones through retirement? Nothing to worry about as we hang over the rail of that imaginary 40-foot sailing yacht making headway toward Key West. Nothing to worry about—from a financial perspective, anyway.

Sound good? Sure it does. But you don't have a pension, and it's too late to start another job and become "vested" in one. What do you do?

Most likely, you already know where I'm going with this: *You can buy a pension.* You can convert your investible, market-vulnerable funds—savings, CDs, and so on—into a steady income stream for life.

How? By buying a fixed annuity.

Although other types of annuities can also play the role of supplemental pension, fixed annuities most closely mimic the absolutely steady, predictable income stream of a typical pension—assuming they're *annuitized* into an income stream (some may elect to take the accumulated asset as a lump sum and walk away with a larger interest accumulation than otherwise available through CDs and other "fixed" investment vehicles, plus tax deferral).

This chapter explores the landscape of fixed annuities.

Fixed Annuities: The Core Idea

Fixed annuities are, well, fixed. "What's fixed about fixed annuities?" you wisely ask.

The payment stream is fixed. That doesn't mean a fixed annuity pays the exact same amount forever. If it has inflation protection or escalation riders, it can pay more over time.

But within certain well-defined boundaries, you'll know what it is going to pay. It's in the contract. That's the key—the payout is fixed, steady, and known up front when you buy it. Typically the interest rate to be credited is known and declared for a defined period of time, then may readjust but can never go below the stated guarantee in the contract. Some contracts will declare the rate for the entire term.

Just like that pension, really. Only in this case, you buy it from an insurance company.

When you buy a fixed annuity, you pay a premium to the insurance company for taking a risk. The insurance company is taking two main risks when they sell you the annuity. The first is *investment risk.* They, not you, have to invest the money to pay you, and you're under contract to receive it, so if they lose, they must make up the difference. The second is *longevity risk.* If you live forever or something close, they'll have to maintain your payments longer than they expected.

You, on the other hand, get peace of mind. With these risks transferred to the insurance company, you can sleep at night knowing what you'll get.

You get a guarantee against loss of principal from market downturns.

You get a guarantee against outliving your money.

The insurance company takes on these risks but builds a profit margin into the "price" (premium) for the annuity. If all goes their way, they make some money investing your money, and they may make money if you die sooner than expected.

It's a calculated bet, one calculated thousands of times each year. You win with income security; the insurance company wins often enough to make it worth offering these products.

Two Main Flavors: Immediate and Deferred

Fixed annuities come in two main flavors, largely segmented by when they *pay out* (recall the classification of annuities from chapter 9: pay-in, payout, and type):

- *Immediate fixed annuities.* You pay a lump sum ("single premium") to purchase this product, and your stream of income begins promptly after that payment. Usually, your payout starts within 30 days after your purchase and is a fixed monthly sum, although it can be annual, biannual, or something else depending on the contract. Such annuities are like an immediate pension—you give a lump sum in exchange for an immediate payment stream for a contracted number of years or life.

  Other names you'll frequently see for immediate annuities include *income annuity, immediate annuity, single premium immediate annuity* (*SPIA*), and *immediate pay* annuity.
- *Deferred fixed annuities.* With this type of annuity, you make a premium payment and deliberately delay the date at which you can start to receive a stream of income. During the deferral period, your money grows tax-deferred. These annuities can be used to put a pension-like plan in place and have payouts start at a flexible date in the future and to build up that "pension" through the modest returns afforded by interest payments received annually before the start date. The owner maintains the flexibility of taking a lump sum at the end of the surrender period and forgoing the regular pension-like payouts. These annuities can be purchased with either a lump-sum payment or fixed or flexible contributions over the accumulation period or both.

These annuities may also be called fixed rate deferred annuities or multiyear guaranteed annuities.

In both cases, you receive guaranteed income now or in the future—unless you choose a lump sum payout. With deferred fixed annuities, you also get some growth, which is largely predefined by the interest rate assigned to the annuity at purchase. Depending on the contract, that interest rate may be *reset* after a given number of years. You should read the reset provisions carefully.

When you receive income, if the annuity was purchased with after-tax ("nonqualified") funds, part of your payout is considered return of principal and is not taxed. The exact portion untaxed can be known up front and is determined by the *exclusion ratio,* which takes into account the portion of a payment that is return of principal versus taxable income. With today's low interest rates, the majority of most annuity payments is return of principal, so tax impacts are relatively light.

How Fixed Annuities Work

The nice thing about fixed annuities is that you'll know up front what you're going to receive and when. What you see is what you get. So how does the insurance company determine what you'll get from a fixed annuity?

In general, the amount of your payout is determined by several factors:

- *Duration of payout.* Contracts may be for a lifetime or for a certain number of years after payments start.
- *Current or contractual interest rate.* Interest rates affect both immediate and deferred annuities but matter more for deferred annuities. Interest rates are set for the accumulation period on a deferred annuity and may be reset according to the contract after a given number of years (read the contract carefully). They will affect the payout, or distribution, period for both immediate and deferred annuities.
- *Time between purchase and the day you start receiving regular payouts.* Obviously, this factor applies for deferred annuities, but it also applies to immediate annuities to a lesser degree, since the first payout must start no more than one year from the purchase date.
- *Your life expectancy.* Life expectancy affects how long the insurer will have to pay and is in turn determined by your age when you start payout and your gender.

- *Your spouse's life expectancy.* This is a factor if you elect to make it a joint survivor annuity.
- *Riders.* These include "period-certain" riders, inflation riders, and so forth.
- *Risk profile of insurance company.* A higher rating could—but not always—mean a lower payment, and vice versa.

As a consequence of all these moving parts, it is difficult to give a rule of thumb for how much a given annuity investment will pay. The "black box" used by the company and its actuaries to calculate your payments is pretty complicated and beyond our scope. Your insurance company and professional agent have the ability to generate real time quotes based on a current situation; these quotes are usually valid for only a few weeks.

That said, you should stick with A/A+ rated companies. The payout amounts will vary according to the company, market factors, and features specific to the annuity.

> Immediate annuity payments are determined by duration of payout, you and your spouse's life expectancy, riders, your insurer's risk profile, and to some degree, by interest rates.
>
> Deferred annuity payments are influenced by all of the above, plus the accumulation period between the time you buy the annuity and payouts begin, and to a greater degree, by interest rates.
>
> Specific payouts are difficult to estimate without a professional quote.

Advantages and Benefits of Fixed Annuities

Fixed annuities have been a "fixture" in the annuities market for years. Advantages include

- *Guarantees, predictability, and no investment risk.* Slip a fixed annuity into your retirement portfolio and—like a pension—you'll assure yourself virtually guaranteed income, for life if you choose, with no investment risk. The insurance company takes the risk; you get the steady reward.

- *Comparatively large payouts.* The "4 percent rule" suggests that you could receive $4,000 per year on $100,000 invested with little chance of running down your principal to zero. A single-premium immediate annuity for someone age 65 should payout something north of that annually, again with no risk of outliving the payouts when lifetime payouts are selected. (Why? Think "sucker factor"—the insurance company can afford to pay you more because it will inevitably pay less to others.)
- *Simple, easy to understand, and easy to buy.* Fixed annuities are straightforward and relatively easy to understand for the average consumer. You pay in, you get paid out. The possible riders add to the complexity a bit. You can buy many fixed annuities (especially immediate) online, but it's still good to have a professional walk you through the riders, help determine how the annuity fits into your overall retirement portfolio, and help select the annuities with the best payouts (they can be quite different because different providers may market more aggressively to different market segments).
- *No ongoing investment or other management fees.* Unlike most investments, especially mutual funds, there are no ongoing fees or costs for a fixed annuity. Once you pay your premium(s), you're done!

> Relatively simple and easy to buy, fixed annuities are predictable, virtually guaranteeing income for life with no investment risk.
>
> Payouts can be larger than comparable investments, and fixed annuities come with no ongoing fees or costs.

Considering the Options

As you think about fixed annuities for your retirement portfolio, you'll have the option to add a number of features to customize them to your specific needs. Here are some of the major categories of riders and benefits you might be offered:

- *Single or joint life.* If you have a spouse it's normally a good idea—unless that spouse has sufficient resources of his or her own—to continue the annuity payments beyond your death to his or hers. Of course, this stretch in payout duration means that payments are reduced depending on the age of the spouse and other terms of the contract.
- *Period certain and refund riders.* You don't want to be suckered by the "sucker factor"—if you pass on the way home from the annuity sales meeting, you don't want to lose all of the principal from your estate. Period-certain (mandatory payments for a specified period) and refund riders (paid in principal in excess of what has been paid out is refunded) make sense unless you have absolutely nobody to leave your wealth to.
- *Inflation riders.* Inflation can eat up the value of a fixed annuity payment stream, especially in the latter years; inflation riders can help preserve purchasing power.
- *Cash withdrawal privileges.* Once you purchase an annuity, your cash is tied up for life for most annuities. That can make it hard to commit funds to annuities, especially if you have limited other savings resources. Cash withdrawal privileges make it possible to retrieve a certain amount of cash from your account, usually a percentage of the initial premium, to handle an unexpected expense while avoiding surrender charges. Most contracts come with a 10 percent annual withdrawal privilege as a standard contract feature (not a rider).
- *Interest rate resets.* With deferred annuities, you may have the option to have the interest rate reset to current rates within specified time periods. If you buy the annuity during a low interest rate period, these resets can help you out. If you want absolute certainty of your eventual accumulation, fewer resets is better.

- *Health and long-term care benefits.* You can add a rider to enhance the payout or provide a lump sum should you encounter a terminal or chronic health problem or if you require long-term care. This may also be a standard contract feature.
- *Legacy benefits.* Finally, in the spirit of period-certain and refund riders, you can purchase a rider to leave a specific portion of your paid-in capital to heirs upon death.

These riders are often included in your contract with no "extra" charge. Always read the fine print—or have someone help you read it.

The (Limited) Downside

Of course, as time has proven again and again, some investments are better than others, but it has also proven that there's no such thing as a free lunch. While fixed annuities offer stability, peace of mind, and often a better payout than the traditional "4 percent rule" would offer, there are a few downsides you should always keep in mind:

- *Annuities aren't risk free.* As presented earlier, annuities are backed by the full faith and credit of the insurance company—and in many cases by state guaranty association funds—but there are no federal or other large-scale protections as found with CDs and some securities. There is some default risk involved, although very few defaults have happened in the past.
- *Inflation can take a bite.* At a 2 percent inflation rate, a $550 monthly payment from your SPIA has only $303 in buying power 30 years down the road—unless you buy an inflation rider.
- *Watch for the "sucker factor."* Again, if you don't protect yourself by adding a period-certain or refund option to a lifetime payout, you (or your heirs) risk losing up to the entire amount of your annuity premium if you die earlier than expected.
- *They're simple, but there's still a lot of detail.* The variations in included features, pay-in and payout schedules and

amounts, and available riders can make even simple immediate annuities a bit complicated. Shop carefully and get help.

Who's Buying SPIAs? Immediate Annuity Hypothetical Case Study

Meet Polly C. Holder. She's single, age 67, and a recent retiree with one grown, self-supporting son. She has Social Security, owns her own home, and has $350,000 in savings accumulated over her lifetime.

She would like to supplement her monthly income to help pay for essential expenses like utilities, food, basic health care, and the like. Polly's healthy and she expects to live longer than the average person her age. Longevity runs in her family; her mother lived to age 91.

She is fairly conservative when it comes to her investment philosophy and is looking for predictable income to last the rest of her life. She doesn't want to worry about what the market is doing and is willing to forgo the potential for higher returns on riskier investments for a portion of her money.

Polly worked with an independent agent who showed her the exact payouts 10 different immediate annuities would generate. The financial strength of the company was important to Polly, so she instructed her agent to only show her companies who were highly rated by the industry rating services.

She decided to put $100,000 into an immediate annuity with a monthly payout of just over $500. Since she used after-tax dollars to buy the annuity, a portion of her monthly payments are considered a return of premium and are not taxable. In addition, if she were to die before receiving at least $100,000 in payouts, the balance would be returned to her son, whom she named as the beneficiary.

Who's Buying Deferred Annuities? Fixed Deferred Annuity Hypothetical Case Study

Mr. and Mrs. Johnson are a retired couple in their early 70s. They have a variety of investments, including a CD that is nearing the end of its five-year term. They were considering renewing it with their bank since they didn't plan on needing it for a least five more years.

The Johnsons' independent agent searched the market and found a five-year multiyear guarantee (MYG) deferred annuity paying almost double the interest rate the bank was offering on the CD. They were also happy to learn that the interest in the annuity would accumulate tax-deferred, unlike their CD.

The Johnsons understood that the annuity was not FDIC insured like the CD, but they researched the insurance company and were satisfied with its company strength and financial ratings. The Johnsons decided to take advantage of the higher guaranteed interest rates and moved the money from the CD to the annuity for the next five years.

A New Idea for Longevity: Fixed Deferred Annuities *After* Retirement

It's no secret that we're living longer these days, and it's no secret that the new longevity brings new challenges to retirement income planning. For years, retirement planners have modeled income needs for 20, perhaps 25 years after retirement. In many cases, they diminished those income needs under the assumption that older retirees would be less active, eat less, need smaller homes, and so forth.

Today's new longevity has changed that thinking. Becoming a centenarian no longer brings you a segment on the nightly local news. Many, many more of us survive well into our 90s. And does that bring with it reduced income needs? Hardly. The amount of daily activity you need help with—from tending the garden to in-home medical care—rises as you reach these ripe old ages.

The upshot is that many of us have enough saved to handle a "normal" 20- to 25-year retirement. But what about that next 10 to 20 years? How will you handle that? Are there guarantees available to cover this "no-go" segment of your retirement? For life, however long that might be?

Fortunately, the answer is "yes." More and more planners are recommending buying a certain type of deferred fixed annuity *at* retirement that starts paying out an income stream perhaps when a client reaches the age of 80 or 85. Such an annuity is obviously less expensive than an annuity that starts paying at 65 and guarantees just the same that you won't outlive your money.

You'll also hear these referred to as *deferred income annuities* or *longevity annuities.*

Make Mine a QLAC, Please

Congress has heard the cry to provide ways to guarantee income for life as we live ever longer and longer.

That's a good thing—because the ways already in place fall short of the mark.

What do I mean? Well, first, it has always been difficult to put an annuity into a qualified retirement plan. Why? Because of annual contribution limits—you can't just dump $100,000 of non-qualified cash into a nice neat deferred annuity for retirement all at once, anyhow. But you can roll over a 401(k), 403(b), or IRA as a lump sum into an annuity—no contribution limits apply.

Second, if you did manage to build an annuity-based nest egg in a retirement account, it was subject to required minimum distributions (RMDs) at age 70 ½ like any other retirement account.

Here's the upshot: If you were intending to use annuities to provide guaranteed income for life starting deep in your retirement—say, at age 80 or 85—it wouldn't work so well.

Congress listened, and in 2014 gave its collective approval to a new concept called a qualifying longevity annuity contract, or QLAC for short.

Here's the idea: Now you can take the lesser of $125,000 or 25 percent of a prior year IRA balance and convert it tax-free into a QLAC. The QLAC is a deferred income annuity (it can't be variable or fixed indexed) that must be set up to start paying at age 85 or earlier. Return of premium and period-certain riders work, so you don't risk losing the balance, and cost of living riders are also allowed.

The main benefit is that there are no RMDs until as late as age 85.

The other main benefit is that you can guarantee income for life—a very long life—with pretax funds.

If you "lack" later-life income security, check into a QLAC.

Who's Buying QLACs? QLAC/Deferred Income Annuity Hypothetical Case Study

Meet Johnny Livelong. Johnny is 68 and is enjoying good health. When he compares himself to his peers, he's confident he'll outlive the average person his age. Like many retirees, he's concerned about outlasting his retirement savings. His assets total $1,300,000, $300,000 of which is his home that he owns outright. He has $500,000 in his IRA account and another $500,000 in various after-tax investments and savings.

Johnny knows that he'll be required to take RMDs from his IRA at age 70 ½, but he would also like to avoid turning on those RMDs if possible. After researching his options, Johnny learns of a new class of annuities called QLACs, which would allow him to delay the start of his RMDs on a portion of his IRA with certain restrictions.

Johnny decides to move $100,000 from his IRA to a QLAC that will begin making monthly payouts to him when he turns 85. Those payouts will continue for as long as he lives and will be substantially larger than payments from an immediate annuity since the money is held for many years before payouts begin.

The QLAC addressed Johnny's two biggest concerns: first, pushing back the RMD start date on a portion of his money and, second, insuring that he would have income for life to address longevity risk.

Johnny also liked the idea that he could potentially be more aggressive with some of his other assets knowing he has the backstop of guaranteed income starting at age 85.

> Deferred income, or longevity annuities, and QLACs can help you guarantee income for extended periods of retirement.

From here, we explore more complex annuity forms, including fixed indexed and variable annuities. Both have features that allow them to grow with the markets and the economy; fixed income annuities are set up to participate in *some* growth while removing downside risk.

CHAPTER 11

FIXED INDEXED ANNUITIES

Why All the Rage?

At long last, you're talking to your insurance agent or financial advisor about annuities. You're pretty jazzed with the idea of a guaranteed income stream down the road in retirement. You have 15 years ahead of you until you retire. You want secure income when that happens and want to "lock it down" during your next 15 years of work. You'd also like to see your nest egg grow some before you retire, not just through your own savings power, but through participating in economic growth. And you'd like to hedge at least a little against inflation.

You talk to your agent/adviser about these concerns. Why lock up money now just to see it grow by very modest interest rates, perhaps not even matching today's inflation rate? You start asking questions. Can I participate somehow in economic growth without risking my nest egg? I know about variable annuities—but I can lose a lot of money on those, right? (Answer: yes!)

These are the right questions to ask, and a good adviser/agent might just beat you to the punch with what has become a very popular answer—fixed indexed annuities (FIAs).

Finding the Best of Both Worlds

You want guaranteed, predictable, and perhaps lifetime income from the annuity corner of your retirement portfolio. You don't want to risk losing any of your principal, but you would like to capture at least some of the returns and inflation protection afforded by a growing investment.

You're willing to give up some of the possible investment returns over time to avoid the risk of losing principal, while locking in gains credited as you go. You want to sleep at night. But when the markets are up 20 percent in a year, you'd like to enjoy a little of that, too.

It's a nice tradeoff. And the insurance industry—which likes to customize products to meet specific and known customer needs—listened. As a consequence, fixed indexed annuities were born. They became popular starting about the year 2000 and have grown to $54 billion in annual sales, or about 23 percent of the annuity market.

Fixed indexed annuities come to market really as an enhancement of the traditional fixed annuities described in chapter 10. They are typically sold as deferred annuities, featuring an accumulation period typically of 5 to 20 years and a payout period usually covered by annuitizing the balance at the maturing date, which is typically retirement age. But they may be set up to start payouts further down the road into retirement, as in the deferred income model described in chapter 10. That said, many indexed annuity holders decide to take the secure tax-deferred accumulation as a lump sum and walk away rather than annuitize.

The key enhancement of fixed indexed annuities is a feature whereby the credited interest, rather than being fixed, can vary *somewhat* according to market performance—that is, the performance of a given market index. Usually the market index is the S&P 500, but others like the NASDAQ 100 can also be used; some annuities track two or more indices.

The word *somewhat* is the key to the previous paragraph. If the market is up, your credited interest rate for that year will be adjusted upward according to one or more variables—usually not fully matching the index gain but sometimes doing so depending on actual index performance and variables, such as caps that may apply. (For example, if an FIA has a 5 percent cap and the index is up 4 percent, the holder will collect the full 4 percent.) If the index has a down year, you are credited with an interest rate floor, which can be as low as 0 percent. But what's important to recognize in those down years is that your principal and any interest credited in previous years is protected.

There you have it. You have gains (albeit not *all* gains) in up markets and some possible flat years when the index is down. And (here's the really good part) *you can't lose principal.*

Modest upside with little to no downside. That's pretty much the proposition—and the pitch.

And why haven't you heard much about fixed indexed annuities? There's a lot of talk about how complicated they are, especially from financial advisors that don't sell them, don't take the time to understand them, and don't like them. Why don't they like them? Could it be because when a client buys one, the advisor loses assets under management and gives up their annual 1 percent fee for managing their money?

Admittedly, some of these products can be complex, and there are many different flavors and combinations of features and tradeoffs to learn about. You should work with an experienced agent or advisor, not do this yourself.

But anyone who is planning ahead for retirement should take a closer look at these products. Fixed indexed annuities can indeed offer the best of both worlds.

> Fixed indexed annuities credit interest based in part on a market index's performance, while at the same time not exposing you to loss of principal when the index preforms poorly.
>
> They offer the best of both worlds; "partial gain with no pain."

Fixed Indexed Annuities: The Core Idea

If you understand fixed annuities (see chapter 10), you're in luck! You are about 85 percent of the way to understanding FIAs!

An FIA is really just a fixed annuity that uses an alternative method to calculate the interest credited to the contract. Rather than treating that interest rate as completely fixed within a reset period, that interest rate can "float" a bit according to market returns for the index it is following. The range of "float" is guided by variables I will describe shortly and may take the rate below the equivalent "fixed" rate in a given (bad) year, but it will *never go below zero.*

Unlike variable annuities, where performance—and thus the value of the annuity—is tied directly to market performance, FIAs are influenced by market performance but not tied to the market directly. So if the markets lose 50 percent in a given year, your credited rate may drop to zero depending on the terms of your contract, but not below zero.

FIAs have minimum guaranteed interest rates (usually 0 to 2 percent) and the ability to convert the money to a lifetime income through annuitization like a fixed annuity. Depending on the contract, both fixed and fixed indexed annuities have surrender charges and penalty free withdrawals (usually 10 percent) and both pass the account value on to a beneficiary at death.

Surrender periods tend to run a bit longer on the FIA to discourage you from pulling the plug early, which can be costly to the company if not enough time has passed for them to cover expenses and profit. Why are surrender charges sometimes longer? Because longer surrender charges allow insurance companies to buy longer-term bonds, which enhance the performance of the contract. Surrender charges also ensure that insurance company losses from selling bonds before maturity are assessed to a particular customer who quit a contract early—not the entire contract base.

Essentially, FIAs blend characteristics of fixed annuities (safety, predictability, steady income) with variable annuities (growth potential) without the downside risks—or most of the costs—of a variable annuity.

While variable annuities are sold and regulated like a security, FIAs are regulated by state insurance departments just like traditional fixed annuities. Securities licenses and registered investment advisor designations are not required to sell FIAs.

> An FIA is really just a fixed annuity that uses an alternative method to calculate the interest credited to the contract.
>
> FIAs blend the safety, predictability, and steady income of fixed annuities with some of the growth potential of a variable annuity without being invested in the market.

How Fixed Indexed Annuities Work

The key to understanding fixed indexed annuities is understanding how the interest rates, which govern what is credited to your account during each accumulation year, are calculated.

With a traditional fixed annuity, interest rates are declared at the beginning of the contract and are locked in for a specified period of time, which could be for one year or more, or through the end of the surrender period. They can be reset at given time intervals defined by the contract but stay fixed otherwise.

With a fixed indexed annuity, the credited interest rate varies according to a formula and a set of defining variables known at the outset of the annuity. Depending on the contract, these variables can also change during the course of the annuity. There are a lot of moving parts to setting these interest rates; I'll introduce you to the variables and follow with a few examples of how an interest rate might be calculated.

For those interested in how the insurance company makes this happen, typically they invest most of the premium paid—perhaps 97 percent—in into high-grade bonds or the equivalent, as in the case of fixed annuities. Then they invest the remaining 3 percent into index derivatives, most commonly index call options, to fund any credited interest rate increases in the case of strong market performance. As I'll describe, you may not get the full amount of the gain because of caps and other limits ("variables") set in the contract. In any case, you'll never lose principal due to a down market, as there is no loss of principal for the insurance company beyond what is paid for the call option contracts, and they bear that risk.

The Defining Variables of FIAs

The interest rate credited in a given year is influenced by three main variables that will be different in any contract you look at. All three variables are used to manage the linkage between the underlying index and the resulting interest rate. All typically attenuate the gain; for example, reducing a 10 percent index gain to something smaller. A contract will typically have *one* of the following and *may* have more than one of the following variables:

- *Participation rate.* The participation rate determines how much of an underlying index gain actually carries over to your interest rate calculation. It's best explained by example: With a 70 percent participation rate and an annual crediting method, a 10 percent gain in the index (say, the S&P 500) will result in a 7 percent interest rate credit to your previous year end contract value. It does not work the same in reverse—that is, a 10 percent loss simply leaves your contract value alone. There is no loss of principal or previously credited interest.
- *Caps and floors.* Many contracts specify a maximum annual adjustment percentage, or *cap,* which can be 3 to 8 percent, and a floor, a level below which the interest rate is guaranteed not to fall (0 to 2 percent, typically).
- *Margin/spread/fee.* These terms cover another adjustor included in many contracts that also serves, like the other two variables, to attenuate or moderate gains. A typical "spread" might be 1 to 4 percent, meaning that a 10 percent gain may result in 6 to 9 percent realized.

The following is an example of how a three-year progression of interest calculations might work out based on given underlying market index gains. With a 70 percent participation rate and a 6 percent cap or a two percent spread, you can see how each of these variables would be applied sequentially over the three years:

- Year 1 = 12 percent index increase
- Year 2 = 6 percent index increase
- Year 3 = (–10 percent) index decrease

Assuming a 70 percent participation rate

- Year 1 = 8.4 percent interest credit
- Year 2 = 4.2 percent interest credit
- Year 3 = 0 percent interest credit *and* no loss of principal *and* no loss of the 8.4 percent and 4.2 percent interest credits in Years 1 and 2

Assuming 6 percent cap

- Year 1 = 6 percent interest credit
- Year 2 = 6 percent interest credit
- Year 3 = 0 percent interest credit *and* no loss of principal *and* no loss of the 6 percent interest credits in Years 1 and 2

Assuming a 2 percent spread

- Year 1 = 10 percent interest credit
- Year 2 = 4 percent interest credit
- Year 3 = 0 percent interest credit *and* no loss of principal *and* no loss of the 10 percent and 4 percent interest credits in Years 1 and 2

So under each of these variables, notice how a 12 percent market gain in Year 1 gets reduced (8.4 percent, 6 percent, and 10 percent). This is the essential tradeoff—the insurance company cuts down the rate but guarantees your principal and interest during the down market years (Year 3). Notice too that the contract can only increase in value, and all interest credited is locked in and cannot be clawed back.

> With an FIA, the interest credited for a given period depends on the performance of the index, the participation rate, the cap, and the spread.

You Are Not Invested in the Market!

It's important to realize that you are never invested in the market. Your insurance company simply tracks the index and credits interest based on how well it did and applies the applicable variables above, which are spelled out in the contract. The markets could drop 37 percent as they did in 2008, and your principal and interest credits will be locked in. You can sleep at night knowing that you'll get some (reduced) gains but never suffer the losses!

Further Understanding the Tradeoff

To fully understand FIAs, a little more clarification on the tradeoff and risk/reward profile would probably help, so here it is.

To have the potential to earn higher interest rates, you are offering a willingness to take a modest amount of a risk. As we've described, the risk is *not* a risk to principal but rather a risk that you may get a lower interest rate in a year when the index doesn't do well than you might have with a similar traditional fixed annuity. That said, the rate will never be negative; no principal will be lost.

It's not a huge gamble, but several years of protracted weak markets can reduce your interest credited to below fixed annuity levels. Your interest rate credit might be zero in total, depending on where the *floor* is set in you contract.

Again—and with emphasis—you'll never lose principal due to a market downturn.

You'll never lose principal with an FIA due to a market downturn. Your risk is that the interest rate might be lower in a given period than a traditional fixed annuity. But it also can be higher if the market index does well.

The Importance of Indexing Methods

The three "main" FIA variables presented above are obviously important in determining how sensitive your FIA will be to changes in the market. Another "moving part" in the calculation is what is known as the *crediting method,* which boils down to the timing and method used to calculate the interest rate change in a certain period. This is typically annual but may be some other interval.

The three most often used methods are

- *Monthly averaging.* The index is averaged by month-end close over a given period, typically a year.
- *High-water mark.* This looks at the index at various points during an interval and takes the highest one. This potentially gives you the maximum possible credit but may be combined with low participation rates and caps and high spreads to render advantages less appealing than they seem.
- *Point-to-point.* This compares the index change to any two discrete points in time as specified in the contract, often annually on the contract date and each anniversary. This can work well if you buy the contract at a particularly low point—but again, watch for "takeaways" in the form of less favorable variables as described previously.

In addition, the *annual reset* feature can be a powerful benefit when the index has a down year; the greater the down year, the greater the benefit. Why? Because not only is your principal protected when the index has a down year, but the contract's starting point for the next year is "reset" to the new lower index value. So you don't have to earn back what the index lost in the previous year before interest can be credited. You'll get credit starting from this new lower index value. Don't overlook the importance of this feature. Any one of these crediting methods can be used with an annual reset.

Other factors that might affect the credit include the interest calculation (simple or compounded) and whether dividends are included in the underlying market index (they're usually not).

Again—shop carefully.

How the Insurance Company Makes Money

To be a smart buyer of any product—and to understand the product—it always helps to understand how the seller makes money and what motivates them to sell it. There are two main ways insurers earn income by selling FIAs:

- *Float.* As with all annuities, the magical Berkshire Hathaway model of earning investment income while the insurance company has your capital is in play. Additionally, because of the way surrender fees and other incentives are set up to keep your contract in force, insurers hang on to your capital longer than with other shorter-term fixed annuities.
- *Higher surrender fees.* As an incentive to keep your contract in force and to not prematurely withdraw more than the annual free withdrawal limit (usually 10 percent), surrender charges can be higher and for longer periods in FIAs than in traditional fixed annuities.

Advantages and Benefits of FIAs

FIAs generally have all the advantages of traditional fixed annuities with a couple additional perks:

- *Some participation in market gains with no market risk.* FIAs by definition allow you to participate to a limited degree in market gains—so you can grow your nest egg and thus your eventual payment stream. But you don't participate directly in the market, thereby eliminating market risk. No FIA owner has lost a single dollar due to market performance. "Gain with no pain" is a good way to describe it.
- *Guaranteed minimum income—plus.* You get the income guarantees for life if you set it up that way and are subject to long-term insurance company solidarity.
- *Traditional fixed annuity advantages—tax deferral and so on.* Beyond the above two advantages, you get all the advantages of a traditional fixed annuity including tax deferral and unlimited contributions. See page 139 in chapter 10.

Considering the Options

Most of the riders that are available for fixed annuities are also available for fixed indexed annuities, such as period certain, health and long-term care, withdrawal privileges, and so on. See the list of riders in chapter 10, page 140.

You can also add special income riders to guarantee a level of income or withdrawal growth. These riders are presented in chapter 13.

The (Limited) Downside

Not surprisingly, there are some downsides to FIAs as compared to traditional fixed annuities—most deriving from some potential for complexity and their moving parts and from how the contracts may be set up. Again, careful shopping can help mitigate these downsides.

- *Returns can be smaller than people expect.* Great market years can happen—then there's a surprise when you open the annual statement for your annuity. Participation rates, caps, and spreads will attenuate your gains; this is the trade-off for protection in down market years. Also, remember that dividends are not usually included when calculating market performance.
- *Resets can change the game midstream.* Many contracts allow the insurer to adjust the variables each term (usually once a year) and before the end of your surrender period. Read the contract carefully and try to find out what that company has done with other contracts in the past.
- *FIAs can actually earn less than fixed annuities.* Bad market years can actually drive interest rates below what you would have gotten with an equivalent fixed annuity—but never below zero.
- *They can be hard to understand.* This may be the chief bugaboo. There can be a lot of moving parts that affect the performance of some of these annuities. Read carefully, ask questions, and look for simple designs.
- *They can have ongoing fees and costs.* Some contracts may stipulate ongoing fees. Typically these are associated with additional riders, most commonly, income riders—check carefully.

- *Early withdrawals and surrender are more expensive.* As I noted previously, insurance companies really want to keep you in these contracts since they are buying longer-duration bonds with most of the money; surrender fees and periods can be larger and longer.

> FIAs offer the advantages of traditional fixed annuities plus an opportunity to increase your interest rate, thus your nest egg and eventual payout.
>
> On the downside, FIAs can be complex and have several moving parts; these parts can cause returns to be lower than the returns of the index it is tracking.
>
> FIAs may have higher fees and surrender charges than traditional fixed annuities.

By Way of Example

For fixed indexed annuities, instead of presenting an example of a purchase choice as I did in chapter 10 for fixed annuities, I thought I'd show how actual FIA returns varied according to an underlying index, in this case, the S&P 500 Index.

Although a bit dated, the following study out of the Wharton School, University of Pennsylvania, illustrates how FIAs can perform around a given index advance or decline for nine six-year periods beginning in 1997 and ending in 2005.

Table 11.1 shows the comparative FIA average return for several comparable FIAs against the S&P return for the period. As you can see, in most years, an S&P loss becomes a gain as the contract is "floored" at certain minimums, while in good periods, like 2002–7, the gain is attenuated (from 13.37 percent to 6.1 percent). You can also see the variance among like contracts as participation rates, caps, and spreads create differences in how credited interest rates are determined.

TABLE 11.1. Fixed Indexed Annuity Returns Compared to the S&P 500: 1997-2010

Period	S&P Index Return (%)	FIA Average Return (%)	Number of FIAs	Return Range (%)
1997–2002	+9.39	9.19	5	7.80 to 12.16
1998–2003	−0.42	5.46	13	3.00 to 7.97
1999–2004	−2.77	4.69	8	3.00 to 6.63
2000–2005	−3.08	4.33	28	0.85 to 8.66
2001–6	+5.11	4.36	13	1.91 to 6.55
2002–7	13.37	6.12	23	3.00 to 8.39
2003–8	+3.18	6.05	19	3.00 to 7.80
2004–9	−1.05	4.19	27	2.25 to 6.83
2005–10	−1.47	3.89	36	2.33 to 7.10

Source: Wharton Financial Institutions Center, Personal Finance, Real World Index Annuity Returns Study, 2010

It Isn't Calculus, So Why All the Confusion?

Listen closely and you'll hear considerable back and forth and differences of opinion among financial advisors and other industry professionals as to the merits and downsides of FIAs. Much of it appears to arise from a lack of understanding of these important annuity products.

Here in this concluding sidebar, I'll attempt to separate the "news from the noise."

The bottom line is that in the end, an FIA is just a fixed annuity that uses an alternative method to calculate the interest credited to the contract. There is simple formula (not calculus) that limits the interest to be credited in positive years.

That limit is the trade-off for locking in the interest credited—interest accumulation that can't be lost in down years. In addition to complete protection of those interest gains, your original principal is also protected when the market index heads south.

Is an FIA a place for all of your money? Of course not—no financial vehicle is.

A fixed indexed annuity can make sense

- to protect a portion of your money from down market years like we saw in 2002 or 2008
- to guarantee income for life (Annuities are the only financial product that can do this. You are basically creating your own pension.)
- if you are near on entering retirement when a single bad year in the market may not allow you the number of years necessary to recover
- if you are looking to have the potential to outperform other conservative options like CDs, fixed annuities and so on, while at the same time protecting your principal from market downturns
- if you are interested in the tax deferral benefits of an annuity
- if protection from creditors is important to you (This varies by state, so check with your legal advisor.)

Who's Buying FIAs? Fixed Indexed Annuity Hypothetical Case Study

Mr. and Mrs. Thompson are in their mid-60s. Mrs. Thompson has retired and Mr. Thompson plans on doing the same in two years. They own their home outright and have accumulated $600,000 over the years in various retirement accounts and personal savings.

The bulk of their money was exposed to market risk during their working years. As they approached retirement, they became interested in lowering their exposure to the whims of the market to avoid the effects a bad year could have on their nest egg just as they retire.

While it was important to the Thompsons to protect a portion of their money from market volatility, they still wanted to try to keep pace with inflation. They were also interested in being able to turn on a lifetime income stream and in knowing today what those monthly payouts would likely be at a chosen future date.

They considered a deferred income annuity, as described in chapter 10. While the payouts were impressive, they didn't think it was flexible enough to meet their needs. The Thompsons wanted the option of deciding later when to turn on the extra income, as they were unsure at what point it would become necessary.

After consulting with their legal, tax, and other trusted advisors, they chose to move a third of the money they had accumulated into a fixed indexed annuity with a guaranteed lifetime withdrawal benefit (GLWB) rider. This and other riders are explained in chapter 13.

The independent agent they worked with researched top-rated insurance companies and showed the Thompsons the exact amounts of monthly income they would receive for life, using various income start dates in the future. They chose a $200,000 annuity. While the rider had an annual fee of less than 1 percent, the flexibility of having a guaranteed lifetime income without having to annuitize was very appealing to the Thompsons.

The money the Thompsons placed in the annuity was protected from market downturns. It would also participate to a degree in a market index's growth years, giving them the potential to keep up with inflation while not being directly invested in the market or exposed to market risk. Through the rider, the Thompsons could know up front what their monthly payouts would be if they decided to turn on their lifetime income at specific dates in the future.

In the end, the Thompsons accomplished their goals of protecting a portion of their nest egg from market volatility, keeping pace with inflation, and adding a flexible way to turn on a guaranteed income stream to last as long as they lived.

With the FIA, they found the best of all worlds.

Currently FIAs are the hottest thing in the annuity market and are enjoying record year-over-year sales growth. Sales hit $54.5 billion in 2015, a 13 percent increase over 2014. FIA sales records have been set each of the last eight years, while variable annuity sales have declined four years in a row.

This is why I laid out the discussion of FIAs *before* variable annuities, which I will cover in chapter 12.

CHAPTER 12

VARIABLE ANNUITIES

Investment Now, Guaranteed Income Later

You want to save for retirement. You want to save during your working years to fill the income gap described in part 1. You want your savings to do some of the work, some of the "heavy lifting," for you. You want your savings to grow during your working years and, if all works out right, to continue growing right on through retirement.

I've described fixed annuities and fixed indexed annuities in the previous two chapters. Yes, your savings grow with these first two annuity types. Your savings grow especially using deferred annuities, which receive *fixed* interest in the case of fixed annuities or *enhanced* interest (enhanced by a link to positive market performance) in the case of fixed indexed annuities (FIAs).

But particularly in light of today's low interest rates, your savings may not grow enough with fixed annuity forms to meet your expectations, particularly when inflation is taken into account. Why? Because you've chosen *not* to tie your savings directly to market performance—and thus not to the growth of the economy. That of course reduces risk, but it may also limit your ultimate retirement income.

However, if you're willing to take some risk with part of your savings in order to enjoy the gains of the markets, you can do so. You can take some risk to grow that nest egg to receive a better payout—either as a lump sum or as a guaranteed payment stream down the road.

That's where variable annuities come into the picture.

An Investment with Insurance Features

Variable annuities are essentially an investment that adds in the insurance features of a guaranteed eventual payout and (usually) a death benefit if you die early. A less secure alternative to fixed annuities, variable annuities have a higher risk for loss but also a higher potential for gain. You control how your money is invested and assume the risks associated with the underlying investments. (With fixed annuities and FIAs, the insurance company assumes that risk.) The growth of your account depends on the success of these investments. Your principal is at risk. Variable annuities have

- *Investment features.* Your money is invested in the markets in a mix of mutual funds of your choosing; the annuity becomes sort of a "fund of funds" working for you. Dividends are received and capital gains or losses directly affect your account balance; the annuity is sold and regulated like an investment.
- *Insurance features.* At the end of the accumulation period, you can annuitize into a guaranteed income stream like a pension; unlike other annuities, the amount available to pay out either as a lump sum or as an income stream may be higher or lower than what you started with—depending on market performance. Most also provide a death benefit that may exceed the actual account value depending on the contract.

These insurance and investment features are rolled up into a single contract sold by the insurance company. Variable annuities can only be sold by an agent with both an investment and an insurance license, so there is both federal and state oversight on sales. Though they are subject to securities regulation, variable annuities are unique contracts and not traded on exchanges.

> Variable annuities are investments with insurance features, including guaranteed income streams and death benefits.
>
> With variable annuities, you get an investment *now* and income guarantees *later.*

Variable Annuities: The Core Idea

A variable annuity is a type of annuity contract that allows for the accumulation of capital on a tax-deferred basis. As opposed to a fixed annuity that offers a guaranteed interest rate and a minimum payment at annuitization, variable annuities offer investors the opportunity to generate higher rates of return by investing in equity and bond mutual funds in grouped subaccounts. If a variable annuity is annuitized for income, the income payment stream will vary based on the performance of the subaccounts.

Variable annuities were introduced in the 1950s as an alternative to fixed annuities, which offer a guaranteed rate of interest. Variable annuities allow you to invest among choices of several professionally managed investments (through subaccounts) consisting of various asset classes, including stocks, bonds, money market funds, and sometimes real estate, commodities, and other specific asset classes. This gives you the opportunity to earn higher rates of return, which can increase the amount of capital you can accumulate and provide an income stream to potentially outpace inflation.

However, you assume the risk of your subaccounts not outperforming the guaranteed return of a fixed annuity—or even losing principal—which can result in less capital accumulation and a smaller income stream upon payout.

How Variable Annuities Work

The following sections present some of the key features of variable annuities.

Subaccounts

When you buy a variable annuity, you can allocate your money among a series of typically six to 12 or more *subaccounts.* Each subaccount typically includes an assortment of mutual funds to choose from aligned with the "style" of the subaccount. The mutual funds act as investment vehicles to gain exposure to the sectors you choose—much like the assortment of mutual funds available in a company 401(k) plan. You can mix and match subaccounts—and funds within the subaccounts—to your liking, weighing toward more aggressive and risky markets or more conservative choices.

Accumulation and Payout Phases

Like most deferred annuities, variable annuities have an accumulation phase and a distribution, or payout, phase. It is also possible to buy an "immediate" variable annuity, giving some growth opportunity during distribution, but these are not common.

During the accumulation phase, you make purchase payments, which you can allocate to a number of investment options. For example, you could designate 40 percent of your purchase payments to bond funds, 40 percent to US stock funds, and 20 percent to international stock funds. The money you have allocated to each mutual fund investment option—and thus the subaccount—will increase or decrease over time, depending on the fund's performance. You can change these choices periodically.

In addition, some variable annuities allow you to allocate part of your purchase payments to a fixed account. A fixed account, unlike a mutual fund, pays a fixed rate of interest. The insurance company may reset this interest rate periodically, usually with a guaranteed minimum.

At the beginning of the payout phase, you may receive your purchase payments plus investment income and gains (if any)—less principal losses—as a lump-sum payment, or you can *annuitize* to receive them as a stream of payments at regular intervals (generally monthly).

If you choose to receive a stream of payments, you may be able to choose how long the payments will last. Under most annuity contracts, you can choose to have your annuity payments last for a period you set (e.g., 20 years) or for an indefinite period (lifetime or the lifetime of you and your spouse or other beneficiary). During the payout phase, your contract may permit you to choose between receiving fixed payments or payments that vary based on current investment performance—that is, the *income stream* can vary, too.

Guaranteed Death Benefit

Most variable annuities have a guaranteed death benefit. Regardless of how the subaccounts perform, a variable annuity death benefit ensures the annuity owner's beneficiaries receive no less than the initial investment. Sometimes they receive more depending on investment performance and other terms of the contract.

Variable annuity investors pay for the cost of that protection through a *mortality charge.* However, this death-benefit protection provides an advantage over investing directly in mutual funds.

Fees and Expenses

Since variable annuities are really professionally managed investment products, there are fees and expenses associated with them that are not associated with other types of annuities. In addition, some of their insurance features carry fees. Specific fees and expenses are described later in this chapter.

Advantages and Benefits of Variable Annuities

Variable annuities allow you to build and maintain an investment diversification suitable to achieve potential growth while also planning for retirement income needs. Like other annuities, variable annuities also provide an eventual lump sum or fixed payment stream—but unlike some fixed annuities, you don't know exactly what that will be in advance. Most variable annuities allow you to take the lump sum or start the income stream when you want or need it.

Other important advantages include

- *Tax-deferred growth.* During the accumulation phase, your investment is not taxed. If your investments grow, tax-deferred status allows you to accumulate a larger balance than in a taxable account. If you have maxed out other tax-deferred accounts, variable annuities provide another avenue for tax-deferred savings.
- *Flexible investments.* Variable annuities allow you to make investment choices and to *change the mix* among those choices. While you can't buy individual stocks, you can choose subaccounts and professionally managed mutual funds to create the portfolio within your annuity. Your return is directly correlated to subaccount performance—up

or down. Most variable annuities offer a representative selection of investments allowing alignment of investments to your risk tolerance.

- *Inflation hedge.* While there is no performance guarantee, history tells us that equities tend to outperform both fixed income investments and the rate of inflation.

Variable annuities allow you to build and maintain an investment diversification suitable to achieve potential growth while also planning for retirement income needs.

Variable annuities offer tax-deferred growth and flexible investment options.

Variable annuities can help hedge against inflation.

Considering the Options

Like other annuities, variable annuities come with an assortment of options and riders to be considered. Many are similar to those already described for fixed annuities and FIAs. Here are a few largely unique to the world of variable annuities:

- *Guaranteed minimum income and withdrawal benefits (income riders).* Guaranteed income and withdrawal benefits, which help mitigate some of the downside risk inherent in variable annuities, are available for most variable annuities at an extra charge. As an example, the guaranteed minimum income benefit (GMIB) guarantees a minimum level of annuity payments, even if you do not have enough money in the account due to investment losses to support that level of payments. These "income riders" are complex but worth understanding if you're thinking of buying a variable annuity. Around 50 to 60 percent of variable annuity owners buy these riders at a 0.5 to 1.0 percent annual cost; they are the subject of chapter 13.
- *Minimum rate guarantees.* For an added charge, some variable annuities offer a minimum floor on the annuity value

even if the subaccounts experience a loss for the year. See guaranteed minimum accumulation benefit (GMAB) riders, discussed in chapter 13.

- *Stepped-up death benefit.* Under this feature, a guaranteed minimum death benefit may be based on something greater than purchase payments minus withdrawals. The benefit is usually based on your accumulated account value as of a specified date. The stepped-up death benefit "locks in" your investment performance, preventing a later decline in account value from eroding the amount left to heirs.
- *Long-term care, periods certain, withdrawal limits, and others.* Like other annuities, features or riders such as long-term care coverage can be added to handle special situations, to guarantee some portion of a payment stream, or to avoid surrender charges (see chapters 11 and 12).

> "Income riders," in the form of guaranteed minimum income or withdrawal privileges, help neutralize the downside risks of variable annuities.

Paying the Freight: Fees and Charges

With other forms of annuities, I've had no need to create a separate section to describe fees and charges. However, with variable annuities, fees are large and complex enough to merit a separate description. Fees and charges can easily add up to 2 or 3 percent of contract value every year and should be understood before purchasing a variable annuity. They help offset the insurer's risks, costs, and sales commissions.

While significant for variable annuities, these fees and charges don't necessarily mean you should avoid variable annuities—you do get value in return in the form of investment potential, death benefits, and other protections with these products.

- *Surrender charges.* If you withdraw money from a variable annuity within a certain period after purchase (typically within six to eight years, but sometimes as long as 10 or even 15 years), the insurance company usually will assess a "surrender charge," which is a type of sales charge. Generally, the surrender charge is a percentage of the amount withdrawn and declines gradually over a period of several years, known as the "surrender period." Often, contracts will allow you to withdraw part of your account value each year—10 percent of account value is typical—without paying a surrender charge.
- *Mortality and expense (M&E) risk charge.* This charge compensates the insurance company for risks it assumes by providing basic death benefits and guaranteed future payments. Typically M&E runs in the range of 1.0 to 1.5 percent per year.
- *Administrative fees.* The insurer may deduct charges to cover record-keeping, preparing statements, and other administrative expenses. This may be charged as a flat account maintenance fee (perhaps $25 or $30 per year) or as a percentage of account value (typically 0.15 percent or so per year).
- *Underlying fund expenses.* Since your annuity subaccounts are typically invested in mutual funds, you'll indirectly pay the costs of managing and administering those funds—typically 0.50 to 1.50 percent annually.

Of course, this list does not include fees for riders or other features like income riders, stepped-up death benefits, long-term care, and so forth.

Downsides and Drawbacks of Variable Annuities

The two primary drawbacks of variable annuities, as compared to fixed annuities and FIAs, are investment risk and fees and charges.

- *Investment risk.* With variable annuities—I can't say it enough—there is risk to principal. The owner is assuming the investment risk, not the insurance company. That risk, of course, is offset by the potential gains.
- *Fees and charges.* These can run up to 2 or 3 percent per year, as already described. This can eat a hole in your investment returns, which may be 5 to 8 percent in a good year. Of course, fees and charges are also assessed in *bad* year.
- *Possible expensive early withdrawals.* Surrender charges are high but can be avoided if you keep the contract through the surrender period. Because variable annuity investment gains are tax-deferred—and because of the way the IRS treats these gains—gains withdrawn are taxed as ordinary income. Withdrawals made prior to the age of 59 ½ may be subject to a tax penalty of 10 percent. As a consequence of these limitations on early withdrawals, variable annuities should be considered as a long-term investment.
- *Limited investment choices.* Through the offered subaccounts, you must choose among the investments offered for your particular annuity. You may have to settle for choices that don't match your preferences or risk tolerance.
- *Tax disadvantages.* While you do get the benefit of tax deferral, you cannot deduct investment losses. Worse, when you withdraw gains, they are taxed as ordinary income—not at the lower capital gains rate—regardless of how long they were held.
- *Lack of liquidity.* If you change your mind about buying a variable annuity—or don't like the investment options or insurance features of the variable annuity you're in—you cannot just ask for your money back. However, you can exchange it for another one using a tax-free "1035 exchange" as described in the sidebar "Don't Like Your 'Old' Annuity? Swap It for Another One." The "1035" can avoid surrender charges if reinvested with the same insurer and can avoid taxes and penalties as well.

Don't Like Your "Old" Annuity? Swap It for Another One

Section 1035 of the US tax code allows you to exchange an existing variable annuity contract for a new annuity contract without paying any tax on the income and investment gains in your current variable annuity account. These tax-free exchanges, known as "1035 exchanges," can be useful if another annuity has features that you prefer, such as a larger death benefit, different annuity payout options, or a wider selection of investment choices.

You may, however, be required to pay surrender charges on the old annuity if you are still in the surrender charge period. In addition, a new surrender charge period generally begins when you exchange into the new annuity. Too, the new annuity may have higher annual fees and charges than the old annuity, reducing your returns.

Here's the bottom line: Shop carefully and exchange carefully.

By Way of Example

Tables 12.1 and 12.2 present a hypothetical example modeled after two annuity choices that might be offered by a large and established insurer. They show the subaccounts available for you to choose from, then the number of mutual fund choices available within each subaccount.

The first variable annuity offering is a pretty typical example (see table 12.1).

TABLE 12.1. Variable Annuity #1

Subaccount (Fund Grouping)	Number of Funds
Asset allocation	8
Domestic equity large cap	14
Domestic equity mid cap	7
Balanced	3
International equity	7
Fixed income	10
Specialty	1 (real estate)
Money market	1

The second variable annuity offers a somewhat broader range of investment choices (see table 12.2).

TABLE 12.2. Variable Annuity #2

Subaccount (Fund Grouping)	Number of Funds
Protected growth strategies	8
Asset allocation	10
Domestic equity large cap	15
Domestic equity mid cap	5
Global allocation	2
International equity	8
Fixed income	15
Specialty	3(*)
Alternative	1
Money market	1

(*) Specialty funds include real estate, global infrastructure, and commodities

You can see from these examples the kinds of choices you have. You can also see (1) the importance of selecting the right variable annuity and (2) the importance of selecting the right investments *within* the annuity.

Making the Determination: Are Variable Annuities Right for You?

When deciding whether to invest in a variable annuity, quite obviously your personal risk tolerance is important. For this portion of your nest egg, can you accept a loss in principal that might "ding" your future payout? The answer for many is "yes," but it is often a good idea to mix a few fixed annuities or FIAs into your portfolio to make sure your income stream indeed matches your needs.

The high costs and fees of variable annuities can diminish returns and exacerbate losses. Make sure you understand the fees and choose an investment mix that will at least cover the fees—otherwise, fixed annuities or FIAs are probably a better choice.

Know that—since a 2007 ruling—financial professionals who sell variable annuities have a duty to advise you as to whether the product they are trying to sell is suitable to your particular investment needs. Don't be afraid to ask them questions. And write down their answers, so there won't be any confusion later as to what was said.

Also know that variable annuity contracts typically have a "free look" period of 10 or more days, during which you can terminate the contract without paying any surrender charges and get back your purchase payments (which may be adjusted to reflect charges and the performance of your investment). You can continue to ask questions in this period to make sure you understand your variable annuity before the "free look" period ends.

Interestingly, but perhaps not surprisingly, variable annuity sales have been declining in recent years as FIAs have gained in popularity. The FIA is simpler and has downside protection and lower fees than the variable annuity. For many, they represent the "sweet spot" between low fixed annuity returns and risky and more expensive variable annuity returns.

As with all annuities, my advice is simple: Read the supporting documents and the prospectus for variable annuities. Understand what you're getting and what it costs and ask questions before you invest.

Who's Buying Variable Annuities? Variable Annuity Hypothetical Case Study

The Andersons are interested in purchasing and annuity and have a financial picture very similar to the Thompsons from chapter 12. They've saved $600,000 over their working years and own their home.

They are both 60 years old and both plan to continue working for at least seven more years. Their two children are grown and doing well financially.

The Andersons have a higher tolerance for risk than the Thompsons and want to have an opportunity to realize higher returns. They understand that with the opportunity for greater returns comes increased risk.

While the Andersons are willing to risk their principal for the possibility of greater rewards, they would also like to set up a safety net that would guarantee a value they could annuitize if they needed to access the money for lifetime income in their later years.

After reviewing available annuity alternatives with their advisors, they decided to put $100,000 into a variable annuity with a guaranteed minimum income benefit (GMIB) rider (riders will be further explained in chapter 13). This rider, as the name implies, guarantees a minimum income base and growth over time, while still allowing the annuity asset value to grow in tandem with the markets if that indeed happens.

While they understood the GMIB rider came with an annual fee of about 0.5 percent, they liked the protection provided in the event their subaccounts did not perform well. What they really wanted was the opportunity to choose subaccounts wisely and meet or even beat market growth rates. This growth—if it went their way—would serve to increase the value and hence the eventual payout of the annuity.

Variable annuities offer a powerful combination of investment and insurance benefits.

With variable annuities, however, your principal is at risk.

FIAs, which are growing in popularity, offer some of the same advantages with less cost and downside risk.

The decision is yours and ultimately based on your risk tolerance. Shop carefully.

CHAPTER 13

INCOME RIDERS

Riding the Gain While Reducing the Pain

You've done your homework. You've read up on fixed, fixed indexed, and variable annuities. You have a pretty good idea of how they work and what purpose they serve in your retirement portfolio. You have a good idea of the virtues and downsides of each annuity type.

Recognizing the importance of growing your assets while you're working, you're intrigued with the long-term asset growth potential of variable annuities. You've read the prospectuses. You're intrigued with the investment options and the ability to choose among them.

But you're dogged with that biggest downside of variable annuities: You can lose principal! And that loss of principal can directly affect what you can receive as regular payments or withdrawals down the road. "What if I invest in a variable annuity, lose principal in a downturn, and pay all those fees on top of that?" you ask. "What would happen to my retirement?"

Good questions. You're on to the scary questions most variable annuity buyers ask. After hearing these questions repeatedly, as is custom, the insurance industry came up with a device—a product enhancement—that, in effect, "insures the insurance." It's a device that, while not protecting the actual asset value of the annuity, protects its income or withdrawal generating potential.

The device is called an *income rider.*

The Core Idea

Income riders are generally sold as an add-on to variable annuity and some fixed indexed annuity (FIA) contracts. The basic idea is this: To avoid the downside risk the markets pose to your annuity's asset base, income riders put a floor on asset value, withdrawal amounts, and/or income gains in the asset base. Thus if the markets go poorly, you'll be guaranteed a set growth rate, withdrawal rate, or minimum asset base, depending on the type of income rider you choose to purchase.

Income riders typically separate a calculated *benefit base* from your actual asset value. Most riders preserve or grow the base according to percentages and formulas set forth in your contract during your accumulation period. That income base is used to calculate your eventual distributions but has no financial value in and of itself.

Because the benefit base—not the actual asset value—is used to calculate your eventual distributions, these riders offer the protection most annuity buyers seek to secure their income streams otherwise exposed to market downturns. I should emphasize that these riders *do not insure the actual asset value of the annuity, but they do insure the annuity's payout potential.* Thus what you can withdraw as a lump sum or leave to heirs is not protected by these riders—only the income streams you can collect through withdrawals or annuitization.

Most riders offer the ability to *step up,* or *reset,* your income base *higher* if markets deliver a specified level of gains. These "step-ups" are permanent; market downturns subsequent to the step-up are locked in and have no effect on your income base.

Income riders typically come at a price of 0.5 to 1.25 percent of the value of the annuity each year through an accumulation period.

Income riders come in different "flavors" depending on the insurance company involved and whether you wish to guarantee a withdrawal dollar amount or percentage of initial investment, an income growth amount, or a minimum asset level for a variable annuity. All three serve to provide the downside protection you seek.

Four Different Flavors

Depending on what kind of rider an insurance company offers, you can guarantee either a minimum withdrawal amount *after* the accumulation period, a minimum growth rate to the income base *during* the accumulation period, a minimum asset level through the life of the annuity, or, in some cases, a combination of the three.

The four flavors of income riders I will cover in the following sections include

- *Guaranteed minimum withdrawal benefits* (*GMWBs*). These guarantee a specific withdrawal amount as a percentage of your initial investment each year.
- *Guaranteed minimum income benefits* (*GMIBs*). These guarantee a growth rate to the benefit/income base during accumulation.
- *Guaranteed minimum accumulation benefits* (*GMABs*). These guarantee that your asset base won't fall below a certain level—often the premium paid in—after a stated period of time, such as 10 years.
- *Guaranteed lifetime withdrawal benefits* (*GLWBs*). These combine the best features of GMWBs and GMIBs—guaranteed income base growth and a fixed and known withdrawal percentage during payout (without annuitization).

Securing Your Withdrawals: The Guaranteed Minimum Withdrawal Benefits Rider

GMWB riders guarantee the ability to withdraw a certain percentage of your initial investment for a set number of years.

When you purchase the annuity with the GMWB rider, a minimum withdrawal amount is established based on a percentage of your initial investment in the annuity. It cannot be reduced even if investment losses reduce the value of your annuity.

While the annual withdrawal percentage stays the same over time—usually 4 percent to 7 percent depending on your age, gender, and other factors when withdrawals start—the *actual dollar amount* of withdrawal may increase (permanently) if the markets rise and the value of the annuity increases. This is called a *step-up*.

Guaranteed withdrawals *do not* require you to annuitize the annuity to start payout, thus preserving your flexibility and control over the annuity asset, including elective withdrawals during the payout period. Although minimum withdrawal amounts are guaranteed, you can start and stop withdrawals as desired.

GMWBs help guarantee ongoing income while preserving your access and control of the underlying variable annuity asset. They also allow you to participate in market growth while avoiding the downside of market losses to your income payouts.

Figure 13.1 illustrates how GMWBs work.

A variable annuity is purchased in Year 0 for $200,000 with a GMWB rider having a 5 percent minimum withdrawal benefit.

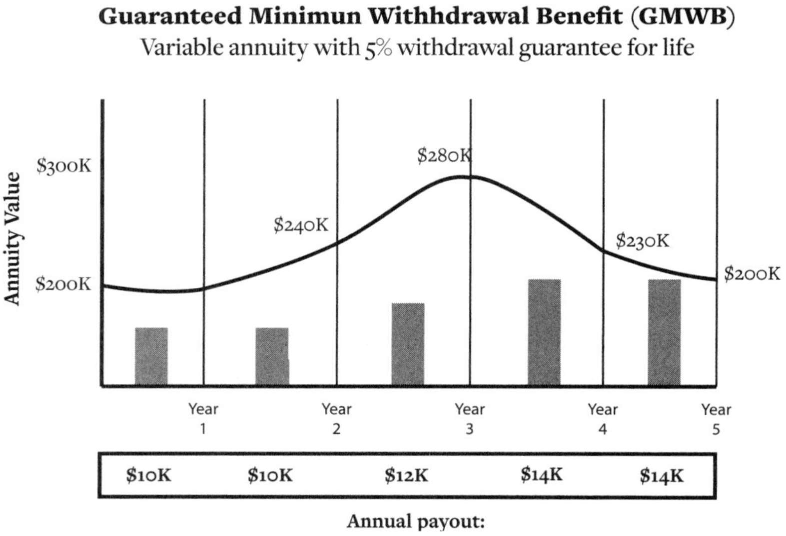

Figure 13.1. Guaranteed Minimum Withdrawal Benefit

The rider guarantees a $10,000 minimum annual withdrawal for a defined number of years. This assumes no elective withdrawals to diminish the annuity balance; deducted annual fees can also diminish the balance and thus the payout.

It's pretty simple to begin with. Then the annuity increases 20 percent in value due to strong market performance during Year 2. The payout percentage, 5 percent, is still applied to the annuity value, producing a step-up to a $12,000 annual guaranteed payout. Such an increase occurs again in Year 3, and the payout increases to $14,000 (5 percent of $280,000), a new floor that will not decrease during the payout period. The guaranteed payout stays at $14,000 even as the markets and annuity value decline in Years 4 and 5.

The costs for these optional riders typically vary between 0.5 and 1.25 percent of the account value annually and are deducted from the account value. Fees are usually based on the larger of actual account value, or the *benefit base*—the imputed value of the account without investment losses. That benefit base, as I mentioned earlier, is not a cash value.

> GMWB riders guarantee a minimum annual withdrawal amount during payout based on a percentage of the initial investment.

Securing Your Income Gains: Guaranteed Minimum Income Benefits

We just saw how the GMWB secures eventual withdrawals from your variable annuity by guaranteeing a percentage of your initial investment to be withdrawn each year during the payout period. We also saw how that amount can increase irrevocably as the market value of the annuity increases.

Another approach to securing payout income and growth is to guarantee the growth in the income, or benefit, base during the accumulation period—regardless of what the markets do. That base, in turn, can be annuitized into a secure, level, and higher payment than what might otherwise be available by simply annuitizing the base annuity. This approach—and this rider—is the GMIB.

By annuitizing on an appreciated income base, GMIBs provide guaranteed, consistent income payments in retirement for a set number of years or for life. The payout is based on a *benefit base*, which is a fictitious amount detached from the actual account value that grows by a guaranteed percentage—the *rollup rate* through a *rollup period.*

The rollup rate usually ranges from 4 to 7 percent annually—5 percent is a good base and one I'll use for the example. With many contracts, the annual rollup can be stepped up by strong market performance, and the benefit base used to annuitize is based on the higher of the actual market value of the annuity or the guaranteed minimum income base.

Figure 13.2 shows a GMIB with a 5 percent rollup rate through a 10-year rollup period.

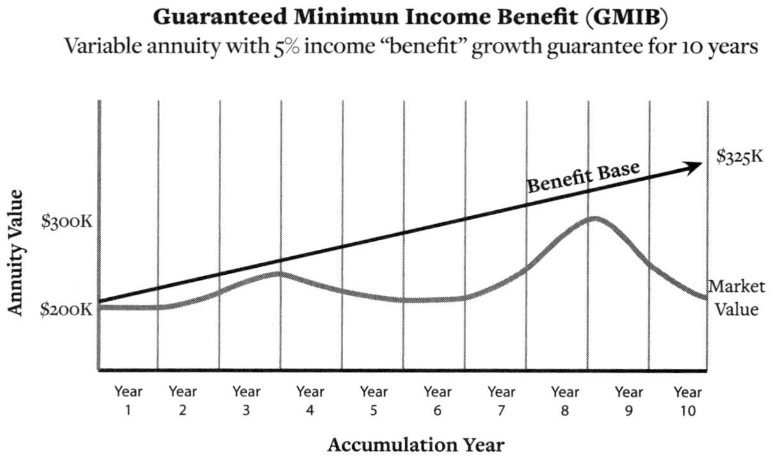

Figure 13.2. Guaranteed Minimum Income Benefit

In this example, an individual invests $200,000 in a variable annuity and selects a GMIB rider offering 5 percent annual *compounded* growth for 10 years. That compounded growth raises the benefit base from $200,000 to just over $325,000 in the 10-year period. When the buyer retires, he or she can annuitize on this value, not the actual annuity value (which remains near $200,000 in this example). Although the cash value ("account value") remains at $200K-plus at the end of the accumulation period, the benefit is based on the $325K amount.

The cost for the rider typically ranges between 0.7 percent and 1.0 percent of the benefit base or account value, often based on the higher of the two. GMIBs assume that the annuity is held intact through the accumulation period and then is annuitized, so this rider should only be used for funds with little chance of being needed for something else.

Now what happens to the GMIB when the market performs well? Figure 13.3 shows what happens to the benefit base with a large market gain in the beginning of the rollup period.

The market gained 50 percent in the first two years (okay, a bit unrealistic, but this is just for illustration). That stepped up the benefit base to $300K, which became the new base for the 5 percent rollup rate over the remaining seven years of the rollup

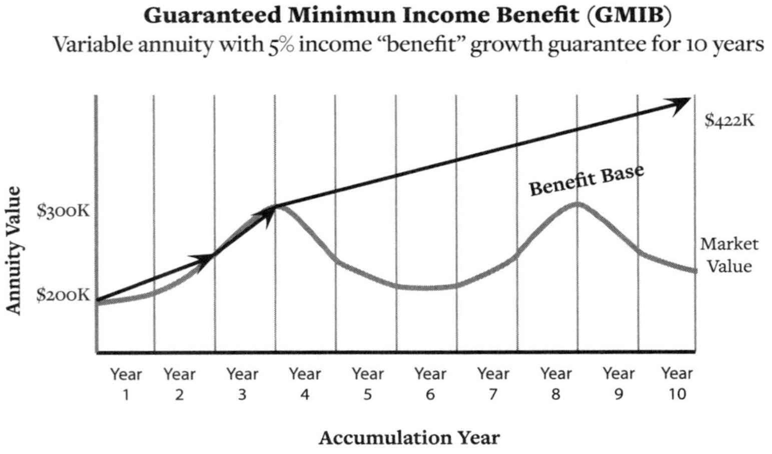

Figure 13.3. GMIB with Strong Market Performanc

period. The new income base is $422K, which will be annuitized over the payout period.

> GMIB riders guarantee minimum growth in a benefit base (not the actual account value) over the accumulation period.
>
> The benefit base is then annuitized for payout.

Securing Your Asset Base: Guaranteed Minimum Accumulation Benefits

The third—and perhaps the simplest—income rider simply guarantees your principal invested will not be reduced by market loss but could increase with market gains. Specifically, the GMAB rider guarantees that at a specified time in the future, your entire principal will be returned to you if the then-current value of the annuity is less than your original investment.

Like the other income riders discussed so far, GMABs allow for market gains to be added onto the minimum base, so you can gain but cannot lose.

GMABs provide for an eventual guaranteed lump-sum withdrawal, not a guaranteed income stream over time as with GMWBs and GMIBs. The actual account value is guaranteed and, of course, can be annuitized. Withdrawals would come out of the guaranteed minimum benefit.

Figure 13.4 shows how the GMAB works with poor and strong market performance.

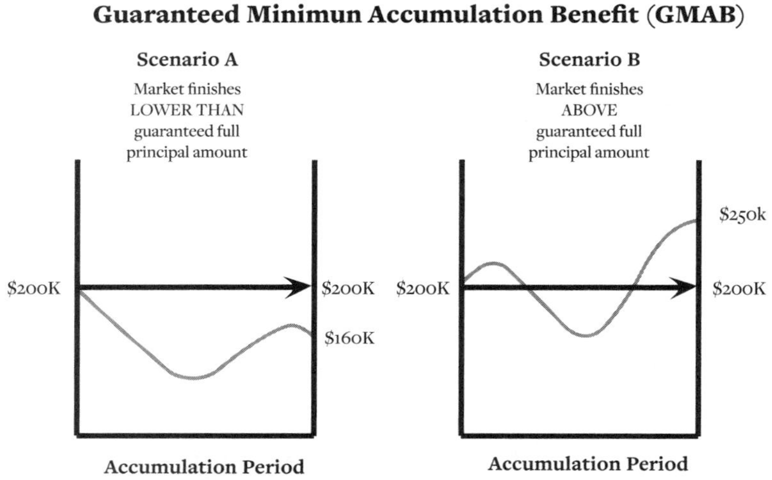

Figure 13.4. Guaranteed Minimum Accumulation Benefit

The costs for GMABs, like other riders, are deducted from the account value and typically vary between 0.5 percent and 1.0 percent of the benefit base or account value, often based on the higher of the two.

> GMAB riders guarantee a minimum principal amount over an accumulation period.

The Best of Two Worlds: Guaranteed Lifetime Withdrawal Benefits

Insurance companies are becoming ever more creative and clever in defining and marketing new annuity products and riders to serve special needs and combine the best among various benefits.

An example is the GLWB rider. This rider is marketed with variable annuities and, nowadays, with some fixed indexed annuities as well.

GLWBs combine the best attributes of GMWBs and GMIBs. They act as GMIBs in the sense that a contractually specified rollup rate is applied during a rollup period to grow the benefit base (again, detached from actual contract value). Then, instead of a mandatory annuitization, the payout is done through a guaranteed percentage withdrawal, much like the GMWB—*with the added benefit that the payouts can be guaranteed for life.*

As such, you get guaranteed income base growth and a guaranteed withdrawal rate with payouts lasting for life but still have access to the actual annuity value through a lump-sum payout and/or through elective withdrawals.

You get the best of both worlds.

How the Insurance Company Makes Money

Again, when shopping for something, it always helps to understand how the seller or marketer earns money from the product and the sale.

Income riders, of course, help remove a lot of the downside risk from variable annuities, which removes one of the biggest sales inhibitors. As such, insurers can sell more annuities and profit from them accordingly in the traditional ways: fees, float, surrender charges, the "sucker factor," and early death upon annuitization under a life-only payout structure.

Insurers also take in cash over time through the additional charges for the rider. Fees of 0.5 to 1.25 percent may not sound like much, but they are applied each year, usually to the higher of the benefit base or actual value. A $200,000 annuity with income riders may produce $20,000–$25,000 in such fees over a typical accumulation or rollup period. Additionally, these riders tend to make keeping the contract until the payout phase look even more attractive. Offering you greater benefits 10 to 15 years into the future coupled with avoiding surrender penalties can be great incentives for you to stick with the contract, all of which helps the bottom line of the insurance company. (This isn't a bad thing. You *want* it to stay in business and thrive—but thrive on someone else's mistakes, not yours!)

None of this is bad—it just becomes part of the value proposition for these riders and annuities in general.

Advantages of Income Riders

The main advantage of all income riders I've discussed is fairly simple and obvious: They provide valuable downside protection because variable annuities without them face the downside risk of bad markets. Income riders guarantee a base for eventual lump-sum withdrawals or annuitization and allow market gains to positively influence that base in most cases.

Income riders not only provide downside protection; they also make your eventual payout far more *predictable.*

> Income riders provide downside protection and upside opportunity and make eventual payouts more predictable.

Disadvantages of Income Riders

The disadvantages of income riders include

- *Cost.* As mentioned previously, income riders can subtly but irrevocably deduct a substantial amount from your account value. They are insurance against downside risk but can be expensive insurance. You pay for this insurance even if the markets gain.
- *Inflexibility.* Many income riders, particularly GMIBs, specify how the eventual payout will occur, mandating annuitization, for example. Income riders can make it more expensive or impossible to take interim withdrawals or an eventual lump-sum payout.
- *Complexity.* Income riders can be hard to understand, particularly when insurers coin their own names or terminology for them. Understand what you're looking at and try to

map what's being offered to the framework I've provided here.

Buying the Rider

I should note here first and foremost that many annuity buyers these days, instead of buying a variable annuity with an income rider for downside protection, opt for the simpler and less expensive FIA. FIAs provide downside protection while also enabling some exposure to market upsides.

The key to buying income riders—just as with the variable annuity itself—is to read and thoroughly understand the contract.

- *Take your time.* Understand what you're looking at; don't make rash decisions.
- *Get outside help.* Have a professional advisor or CPA or some such read the contract.
- *Map out the possibilities.* Get the agent to map out scenarios with specific dollar amounts.
- *Ask lots of questions.* This is self-explanatory.

These tips, of course, apply to all annuity purchases. I'll wrap up my discussion of annuities and their use in retirement in chapter 14.

> When buying a variable annuity with an income rider, understand the detail and how different scenarios play out.
>
> Remember that many buyers these days are opting for FIAs for similar downside protection at a lower cost.

CHAPTER 14

SHOULD YOU BUY AN ANNUITY?

The Bottom Line

We've covered a lot of ground here.

No doubt you bought this book because you're concerned about retirement. You want to make sure all the bases are covered, that you have enough income and assets available during retirement to be comfortable and secure, and that you can meet your standard of living objective while not outliving your money.

Throughout this 14-chapter journey, we've defined the problem (the "Retirement Crisis") and checked into how retirees and their advisors are going about solving it. We've discussed retirement needs and the resource mix of entitlements, pensions, and savings used to meet those needs.

We've emphasized a central theme: Retirement needs have expanded due to longevity and other factors, while retirement resources are declining or are in a state of flux. Traditional pensions are disappearing, Social Security is at risk, and safe returns on savings are ever harder to come by.

As these changes gather momentum, the need to add something to the mix to secure income during retirement has only increased.

That is where annuities fit in—and we've placed special emphasis on annuities in part 2 of this book as a consequence.

In this chapter, I'll review main themes covered so far and offer some additional insights on annuities from my 30 years in the industry.

Understanding the Problem: The Retirement Crisis Revisited

In chapter 1, I defined a "Retirement Crisis" that is making it ever harder to build a "rock-solid," secure retirement footing. Elements of the retirement crisis include

- *Increased life expectancy.* If you successfully reach age 65, you can expect to live to age 86.6 (male) or 88.8 (female)—about 2 years longer than in 2000. By 2050, average life expectancies will be in the 90s for women.
- *Higher standards of living.* Most of us have lived better in the years before retirement than ever. We own our own homes, we own bigger homes, we have more than one car, we travel, we are eating out more, and so on. We carry those expectations into retirement.
- *Higher health care costs.* This requires no explanation, but making it worse is the declining availability and increasing cost of employer retiree coverage.
- *Forced earlier retirements.* Layoffs, job changes, and health issues are forcing many to retire earlier than expected.
- *Disappearing pensions.* Aside from Social Security, defined benefit pensions are the best and most secure retirement resource. But only 18 percent of today's private employers offer one, and even the heretofore secure public sector pension is becoming less secure.
- *Social Security concerns.* Social Security is the best retirement income resource available. But the problem is, it's far from enough, and although not likely, necessary changes could reduce the benefit even further.
- *Inflation.* We don't think so much about inflation these days, as the crisis years in the late 1970s and early 1980s are far behind us and inflation seems well under control. Yet even

at today's low 1 to 2 percent rates, 30 years of retirement (there's longevity working against us again!) can really diminish purchasing power.

- *Unhelpful markets.* While the stock markets have historically provided a vehicle to grow savings and beat inflation, they have become more volatile in recent years. And fixed income in the form of savings, CDs, and most bonds don't even keep up with inflation. Growing savings for retirement means taking more risks than ever.

So, in sum, there is more to accomplish to achieve a secure retirement—and fewer secure ways to accomplish it.

Bottom line: Retirement requires more careful planning than ever.

Where Annuities Fit into the Plan

Annuities have been around since the time of the Romans. Okay, it wasn't like the modern form of annuities available to ordinary individuals like you and me to supplement retirement.

But it's an old idea—pay a sum up front or in installments, watch it grow, then let it pay you back an income stream that can last as long as you want. While some use annuities strictly as vehicles to achieve tax-deferred growth, most look at annuities as an instrument to provide predictable, steady income for a definite period in retirement or, even better, for life, to account for the insecurity of longevity and the vagaries of fluctuating asset values. In short, annuities provide security and make it harder to outlast your money.

In most retirement plans, annuities fill the gap once filled by pensions. Instead of adding a pension to Social Security to round out a secure retirement income, many individuals now use savings—often from rolled over retirement plans—to buy annuities, converting an asset into a secure income stream. Figure 14.1, also presented in chapter 1, illustrates this.

Note that "Savings" are still part of the mix. You should never deplete all your savings to buy annuities because you may need those savings to meet unexpected needs.

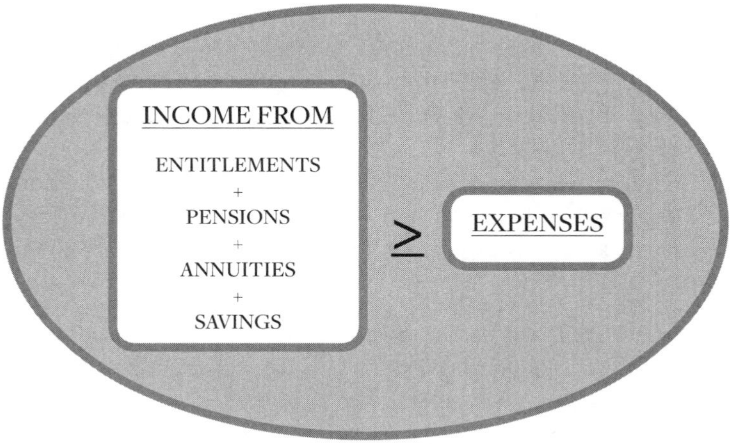

Figure 14.1. Enhanced Retirement Planning Model, Including Annuities

A typical retirement income plan might consist of 40 percent Social Security, 30 percent annuities (annuity income), and the remaining 30 percent in savings. These percentages will vary according to your Social Security eligibility and the amount and variability of your retirement needs. If your home is paid off, for instance, you may need less steady income.

Bottom line: Annuities should be considered for your total retirement resource portfolio and probably make sense for a fraction of it. The size of that fraction will vary.

A $64,000 (or More) Question:
Should *You* Buy an Annuity?

In the last section, I revisited the role annuities play in a typical retirement plan. But that doesn't address a central question directly: Should *you* buy an annuity?

Obviously, there is no "pat" answer to this question. You are an individual with individual needs, risk tolerance, and ability and willingness to manage your own funds through retirement. And there are many types of annuities serving different needs and risk tolerances. So the real bottom line is that it depends on who *you* are and what *you* need—and what type of annuity we're talking about.

That answer seems to beg the question. But a few common guideposts can help you decide if an annuity is right to consider for a portion of your retirement portfolio. I'll share them here:

- You're looking for steady, predictable income—guaranteed for life—and are willing to give up at least some possible market gains to get it.
- You're fearful of outliving your assets.
- You want to worry less about market performance.
- You want to diversify your retirement portfolio beyond traditional market investments.
- You want to hand off some of the risk, time, and effort to manage your assets to someone else.
- You want to add tax-deferred savings beyond traditional IRA, 401(k), and other contribution limits.
- You want to shelter some savings from legal liability.

If these guideposts speak to you, it's time to start shopping!

Shop 'til You Drop: How to Buy an Annuity

Just as there are many companies you can invest in, or many kinds of cars you can buy, there are a great many annuities available. And like cars and companies, some are better suited for you than others.

Buying an annuity is a shopping process similar to that for any big-ticket item. First, you need to understand what you need. You need to know at least a little about the "product" going in. You need to engage with a knowledgeable professional/salesperson/agent licensed to describe the features and make the sale. You need to consider the alternatives carefully, read the fine print, think through the benefits and costs, and make a careful decision.

Talk to the Professionals

Annuities are products. They are products that must be sold by licensed professionals. Most annuities are sold by insurance companies through licensed insurance agents; these professionals must also be securities licensed if selling variable annuities.

Most financial advisors and investment brokers are not licensed to sell annuities. "Fee-only" advisors cannot collect commissions for selling them. As a consequence, remember that such professionals may not discuss annuities—though they may make sense—because they can't sell them. And if you buy an annuity, these investment advisors would lose the ability to manage the assets committed to the annuity. This "channel conflict" keeps many individuals out of annuities where they might otherwise make sense.

Be aware that annuity sales professionals do get commissions and get larger commissions for selling certain types of annuities—some fixed indexed annuities and variable annuities in particular. That shouldn't deter you from listening to their presentations, which are usually quite interesting and informative. But you should understand this bias and work with a professional you trust to look after *your* needs first.

To counteract this possible bias, and to better understand what you're buying, it's a good idea to get someone else involved, like a friend or, even better, another financial professional—your CPA or tax advisor, for instance. Many people look for outside confirmation and help when buying a car—why wouldn't you do the same for a product that provides a significant portion of your retirement?

Also, be sure to work with an independent agent who has access to many companies and annuity products. An agent representing one company with access to only a few annuities to offer isn't as likely to have the best fit for your needs and situation as compared to an agent who has access to, say, 25 companies and their products, giving many more options to choose from.

Bottom line: Find a professional you can trust, prepare, listen carefully, and get more help.

Be Aware of the Pros and Cons

I've been examining pros and cons of annuities and different forms of annuities throughout the book and especially in part 2. Here, for review, is a summary (not all of these apply to all types of annuities):

Pros

- steady, predictable income in retirement
- tax-deferred growth
- no market risk (except variable annuities)
- flexible payouts (annuitize or lump sum), many with free elective withdrawals
- configurability (varied products and riders)

Cons

- restricted access to savings (surrender periods and charges)
- difficult to change (but not impossible) once bought
- fees and costs (some more than others)
- guaranteed by longevity of insurance company, no federal insurance (e.g., FDIC or SIPC)
- detail and complexity

If you keep these pros and cons and how insurance companies make their money—fees, float, surrender charges, and "sucker factor" (premature death)—in mind, you'll be able to carry on a better conversation with the annuity professional.

Remember also that by choosing the annuity that's right for you, you can avoid or reduce the effects of the "cons"—for example, don't invest funds you might need in five years in an annuity with a 10-year surrender period.

Bottom line: Like any big-ticket purchase, knowing the pros and cons will make you a smarter annuity buyer.

Know What the Naysayers Say

Starting with the investment and financial advisors who don't sell them, there are a lot of vocal naysayers out there in the media and advertising world. Most are trying to convince you that annuities are evil and should be avoided at all cost. I always like to present the counterargument because it helps you understand the argument!

Here's (some of) what they have to say:

1. The charges and fees are too high!

Many times, the naysayers lump all annuities together when discussing the cons. For example, the charges and fees they're citing are associated only with variable annuities and their subaccounts and riders—high fees and charges don't apply to all annuities.

The other fee that draws attention is the surrender fee. What's sometimes overlooked is that this charge is avoidable by keeping the contract in place through the surrender period and not exceeding the typical 10 percent free withdrawal privilege available in most contracts.

Eventually the surrender fee goes away, never to be paid! It's in place to recover losses and costs (such as sales commissions) incurred by the insurance company if you were to end the contract early. But again, keeping the contract until the surrender period is over puts you in the position of never having to pay a surrender fee. This is quite different from charges you may encounter with some investments that take an annual fee for as long as you are in the investment.

2. There is no liquidity!

Annuities are long-term propositions. You should not commit more money to a deferred annuity than you are comfortable not being able to access during the surrender period.

This can be avoided with shorter three- to five-year surrender period products and products that offer an annual penalty-free withdrawal provision (usually 10 percent) during the surrender period. Other provisions or riders can allow for greater access for long-term care needs and other events.

No credible agent will tell you to put all of your money into an annuity. Liquidity varies widely among annuity types and from company to company. Look for the annuity that fits your needs.

As with most analyses, you must consider the source. What do these naysayers have to gain by taking the "all annuities are bad" stance? Often it boils down to the fact that if you were to move money into an annuity, the advisor (and probable commentator)—who doesn't sell them—loses income. When a client purchases an annuity, it removes assets from the pool of investments that the advisor manages, shrinking the pool of money from which his or her annual fee is calculated.

As you can see, I'm a proponent of annuities as part of a well-rounded retirement income strategy. But I realize that different people have different needs, and other investment choices are also important.

Remember, Not All Annuities Are Alike

Different annuities serve different purposes. An immediate fixed annuity converts a savings sum directly into an income stream right now, while a variable annuity provides long-term, tax-deferred growth to gain a bigger income stream later. Fixed indexed annuities do that too, but don't tie directly to market performance, while also offering downside protection.

Through the large assortment of riders available, you can make an annuity do pretty much what you want it to. You can make it safer, you can make it deal with a change in your circumstances (medical or long-term care), and so on. And remember this: Annuities are products, and insurance companies are marketers. Different companies have different specialties and use pricing differently to achieve market-share objectives. One insurance company might offer a much better package for a particular type of annuity than another—better payout, better features, better riders, lower costs. I've seen 20 to 30 percent variations in costs, payouts, and so on, from one company to the next; I've even seen good-sized differences between two annuities of the same type offered by the same company!

Bottom line: Different annuities serve different needs in your retirement resource portfolio. Shop carefully!

Thus . . .

You Don't Have to Buy Just One Annuity

You may choose to buy a variable annuity with an income rider now to achieve tax-deferred growth and likely a larger payout later than a comparable fixed annuity. You can buy a variable annuity (VA) or a fixed indexed annuity (FIA) now; then, depending on its performance, buy an immediate fixed annuity later at retirement to supplement the VA *if needed*. The VA or FIA supplements your other retirement resources; the immediate annuity supplements the VA and FIA.

It's always good to plan your annuity portfolio *within* the annuity bucket *within* your retirement portfolio. Different needs, and different strokes for different folks. And remember, you don't have to buy them all at once.

Bottom line: Not all of your annuity eggs should be put in one basket or purchased at the same time.

Get the Details Right

This bears repeating: Know what you're buying before you buy it. Read the details. Read the prospectus. Have the annuity professional walk you through the prospectus. Have him or her walk you through different scenarios. Get help from friends. Make sure the assumptions are realistic—no 8 or 10 percent annual market returns, please!

You can't know enough. It might be the most important purchase decision for at least the retirement portion of your life. Study carefully and get help.

Bottom line: Make the effort to understand the detail and scenarios behind any annuity purchase.

It's All About You

Really, it is. We still exist in a "legacy" period where a few bad actors have poisoned the well by aggressively selling annuities that might not have been right for people to generate large commissions for themselves.

The world is changing. We have more consumer protection. An annuity salesperson is required to be licensed in every state where he or she sells annuities, with continuing education requirements. Agents must complete product-specific training for every annuity they sell.

In recent years, most states have expanded consumer protection by adopting regulations regarding suitability in annuity transactions. The agent must have reasonable grounds to believe the recommended annuity is suitable for the customer. Carriers must also do a secondary suitability review of every annuity transaction before issuing a contract.

Everyone involved in marketing annuities has a duty to uphold the integrity of the industry, and many agents have taken that to heart all along. But greed is greed, and there are still sharks in the water.

As a consequence, be demanding! While these consumer protections help, there is a lot of gray area in defining "suitable." Make sure what you're buying is really suited to your needs, risk tolerance, and expectations. Read and study carefully, ask lots of questions, get it right, and make your professional get it right.

Finally, remember that annuities frequently come with a return of premium guarantee, which provides consumers with a "free look" period after receiving the contract. As buyer, you can return the contract for any reason—even if you don't like the color of paper it's printed on!—within a specified number of days (usually 10 or more) for a full refund.

Best wishes for a secure, comfortable retirement to you and your family.

> Bottom line: This annuity is for you! Make it yours. Don't accept second best.

Watch Out! Ten Common Annuity Pitfalls

Finally, I'll share 10 annuity "pitfalls" I've assembled from my 30 years of collected wisdom. It helps to know what to do by knowing *what not to do.* These are in no particular order:

1. *Don't learn the hard way that not all insurance companies are created equal.* When entering into an annuity contract that involves a long payout window, you're striking an important relationship that will stretch to the end of your days (and beyond, for surviving family members). So you'll want to do plenty of research to find out how long the company has been in business, what its financial situation is, and what complaints may have been lodged against it through the Better Business Bureau, state insurance regulators, and so on.
2. *Don't rely on just one annuity.* You never want to put your annuity "eggs" in one basket. Instead, splitting your savings into multiple annuities with varying strategies helps protect against a worst-case market scenario.
3. *Don't buy an annuity you don't understand.* If you're buying any product you're not 100 percent sure of, your agent hasn't done his or her job. Never purchase an annuity until you're exactly sure how it works, how income is paid back to you, and what your options are for withdrawals and passing in on to your heirs.
4. *Don't underestimate market risk.* If your annuity's return is based on the market, your payments can and will fluctuate. You should determine how much market risk you're willing to take and how much your annuity market risk overlaps with other market risk in your retirement portfolio. The goal is never to be caught short on income needs in retirement—so the more that income stream depends on the whims and winds of the market, the bigger the chance you're taking.
5. *Figure out tax implications beforehand.* Annuities are given tax-deferred status; the money you put in or earn isn't taxed until it's withdrawn. But on withdrawal, the

money received that is not considered a return of principal is taxed as ordinary income, not as capital gains. Talk to an accountant or tax advisor if you have a complex tax situation and are considering annuities.

6. *Don't overdo the riders.* Riders are annuity amendments that provide a protection or benefit in exchange for a payment or fee in most cases. They help you tailor the annuity to your needs; however, they can load a lot of cost onto the annuity. Make sure the rider is really necessary and worth the costs. If a rider costs 0.5 percent ($500 a year on a $100,000 annuity) annually, try to imagine yourself paying for that with real cash. Is it worth it?
7. *Be careful when talking to agents representing only one insurance company.* One carrier is not the perfect fit for every situation. With an independent agent who offers multiple products from multiple companies, the chance for finding a good fit is much better.
8. *Understand the proper time horizon.* If you're looking for a place to put money for two to three years, an annuity is probably not the thing for you. Most annuities are long-term contracts with substantial penalties for early withdrawal.
9. *Be honest about how much liquidity you'll need.* Don't enter into a deferred annuity if you're unsure whether you can live without that money immediately. On top of surrender charges, the IRS will slap on a 10 percent penalty if you withdraw money before age 59 ½.
10. *Factor your age into the equation.* If you're younger than 40 and looking at annuities, you don't want to sock away large sums representing a significant portion of your retirement nest egg. Why? Because of early withdrawal penalties. Use annuities for a small growth "corner" of your portfolio and add to that "corner" over time.

Follow these 10 guideposts and you'll stay out of trouble and make the most of your annuity purchase.

APPENDIX A

Ratings and What They Mean

A.M. Best ratings

Rating:	Descriptor:	Definition:
A++, A+	Superior	Able to meet insurance obligations.
A, A-	Excellent	Able to meet insurance obligations.
B++, B+	Good	Able to meet insurance obligations.
B, B-	Fair	Vulnerable to unfavourable economic conditions.
C++, C+	Marginal	Vulnerable to unfavourable economic conditions.
C, C-	Weak	Very vulnerable to unfavourable economic conditions.
D	Poor	Extremely vulnerable to unfavourable economic conditions.
E	Under Supervision	Company is under regulation, preventing normal business operations.
F	In Liquidation	Company is ongoing voluntary liquidation.
S	Suspended	Unevaluated due to inadequate information or lack of cooperation.

Moody's ratings

Rating:	Descriptor:	Definition:
AAA	Extremely Strong	Market conditions are unlikely to affect a fundamentally strong positions.
AA	Very Strong	High-grade company with marginally larger long-term risks.
A	Strong	Financially secure, but signs of possible long-term susceptibility.
Baa	Adequate	Lacking in certain protective elements over the long term.
Ba	Questionable	Ability to meet obligations is questionable.
B	Poor	Long-term ability to meet obligations is small.
Caa	Very Poor	May be in default of financial obligations already.
Ca	Extremely Poor	In default of financial obligations.
C	Extremely Poor	Very poorly positioned to offer financial security.

S&P ratings

Rating:	Descriptor:	Definition:
AAA	Extremely Strong	Very unlikely to be affected by adverse economic conditions.
AA	Very Strong	Unlikely to be affected by adverse economic conditions.
A	Strong	Marginally more likely to be affected by adverse economic conditions.
BBB	Good	May be affected by adverse business conditions.
BB	Marginal	Adverse business conditions may lead to inability to meet obligations.
B	Weak	Adverse business conditions are likely to affect ability to meet obligations.
CCC	Very Weak	Depends on favourable business conditions to meet obligations.
CC	Extremely	Likely to not meet all financial obligations.
R	Regulartory Action	Subject to regulation due to insolvency.
NR	Not Rated	No opinion

Fitch ratings

Rating:	Descriptor:	Definition:
AAA	Exceptionally Strong	Very unlikely to be affected by adverse economic conditions.
AA	Very Strong	Not significantly vulnerable to adverse economic conditions.
A	Strong	Low expectation for interruption of pay.
BBB	Good	May be affected by adverse exonomic conditions.
BB	Moderately Weak	Contractual obligations are now vulnerable.
B	Weak	Significant risk for interruption of payments.
CCC	Very Weak	Significant likelihood for interruption of payments.
CC	Extremely Weak	Interruption of payments is probable.
C	Distressed	Interruption of payments is imminent.

APPENDIX B

Life Expectancy Tables

Life expectancy at birth, at age 65, and at age 75, by sex, race and Hispanic origin:
United States, sellected years 1900-2013

Updated data when available, Excel, PDF, and more data years: http://www.cdc.gov/nchs/hus/contents2014.html016

[Data are based on death certificates]

Specified ages and year	All races			White			Black or African American		
	Both sexes	*Male*	*Females*	*Both sexes*	*Male*	*Females*	*Both sexes*	*Male*	*Females*
At birth									
1900	47.3	46.3	48.3	47.6	46.6	48.7	33.0	32.5	33.5
1950	68.2	65.6	71.1	69.1	66.5	72.2	60.8	59.1	62.9
1960	69.7	66.6	73.1	70.6	67.4	74.1	63.6	61.1	66.3
1970	70.8	67.1	74.7	71.7	68.0	75.6	64.1	60.0	68.3
1980	73.7	70.0	77.4	74.4	70.7	78.1	68.1	63.8	72.5
1990	75.4	71.8	78.8	76.1	72.7	79.4	69.1	64.5	73.6
1995	75.8	72.5	78.9	76.5	73.4	79.6	69.6	65.2	73.9
2000	76.8	74.1	79.3	77.3	74.7	79.9	71.8	68.2	75.1
2001	77.0	74.3	79.5	77.5	74.9	80.0	72.0	68.5	75.3
2002	77.0	74.4	79.6	77.5	74.9	80.1	72.2	68.7	75.4
2005	77.6	75.0	80.1	78.0	75.5	80.5	73.0	69.5	76.2
2006	77.8	75.2	80.3	78.3	75.8	80.7	73.4	69.9	76.7
2007	78.1	75.5	80.6	78.5	76.0	80.9	73.8	70.3	77.0
2008	78.2	75.6	80.6	78.5	76.1	80.9	74.3	70.9	77.3
2009	78.5	76.0	80.9	78.8	76.4	81.2	74.7	71.4	77.7
2010	78.7	76.2	81.0	78.9	76.5	81.3	75.1	71.8	78.0
2011	78.7	76.3	81.1	79.0	76.6	81.3	75.3	72.2	78.2
2012	78.8	76.4	81.2	79.1	76.7	81.4	75.5	72.3	78.4
2013	78.8	76.4	81.2	79.1	76.7	78.8	75.5	72.3	78.4

At 65 years									
1950	13.9	12.8	15.0	14.1	12.8	15.1	13.9	12.9	14.9
1960	14.3	12.8	15.8	14.4	12.9	15.9	13.9	12.7	15.1
1970	15.2	13.1	17.0	15.2	13.1	17.1	14.2	12.5	15.7
1980	16.4	14.1	18.3	16.5	14.2	18.4	15.1	13.0	16.8
1990	17.2	15.1	18.9	17.3	15.2	19.1	15.4	13.2	17.2
1995	17.4	15.6	18.9	17.6	15.7	19.1	15.6	13.6	17.1
2000	17.6	16.0	19.0	17.7	16.1	19.1	16.1	14.1	17.5
2001	17.9	16.2	19.2	18.0	16.3	19.3	16.2	14.2	17.7
2002	17.9	16.3	19.2	18.0	16.4	19.3	16.3	14.4	17.8
2005	18.4	16.9	19.6	18.5	17.0	19.7	16.9	15.0	18.3
2006	18.7	17.2	19.9	18.7	17.3	19.9	17.2	15.2	18.6
2007	18.8	17.4	20.0	18.9	17.4	20.1	17.3	15.4	18.8
2008	18.8	17.4	20.0	18.9	17.5	20.0	17.5	15.5	18.9
2009	19.1	17.7	20.3	19.2	17.7	20.3	17.8	15.9	19.2
2010	19.1	17.7	20.3	19.2	17.8	20.3	17.8	15.9	19.3
2011	19.2	17.8	20.3	19.2	17.8	20.4	18.0	16.2	19.4
2012	19.3	17.9	20.5	19.3	18.0	20.4	18.1	16.2	19.5
2013	19.3	17.9	20.5	19.3	18.0	20.5	18.1	16.3	19.5
At 75 years									
1980	10.4	8.8	11.5	10.4	8.8	11.5	9.7	8.3	10.7
1990	10.9	9.4	12.0	11.0	9.4	12.0	10.2	8.6	11.2
1995	11.0	9.7	11.9	11.1	9.7	11.9	10.2	8.8	11.1
2000	11.0	9.8	11.8	11.0	9.8	11.8	10.4	9.0	11.3
2001	11.2	9.9	12.0	11.2	10.0	12.0	10.5	9.0	11.5
2002	11.2	10.0	12.0	11.2	10.0	12.0	10.5	9.1	11.5
2005	11.5	10.4	12.3	11.5	10.4	12.3	10.9	9.4	11.2
2006	11.7	10.6	12.5	11.1	10.6	12.5	11.1	9.1	12.0
2007	11.9	10.7	12.6	11.9	10.8	12.6	11.2	9.8	12.1
2008	11.8	10.7	12.6	11.8	10.7	12.6	11.3	9.8	12.2
2009	12.1	11.0	12.9	12.1	10.4	12.9	11.6	10.2	12.5
2010	12.1	11.0	12.9	12.1	10.6	12.9	11.6	10.2	12.5
2011	12.1	11.1	12.9	12.1	10.8	12.9	11.7	10.4	12.5
2012	12.2	11.2	12.9	12.1	11.2	12.9	11.8	10.4	12.7
2013	12.2	11.2	12.9	12.1	11.2	12.9	11.8	10.4	12.7

APPENDIX C

Annuity State Guarantee Protection Limits

Alabama	$100,000
Alaska	$100,000
Arizona	$100,000
Arkansas	$300,000
California	$80,000
Colorado	$100,000
Connecticut	$100,000
Delaware	$100,000
District of Columbia	$300,000
Florida	$100,000 - $300,000
Georgia	$100,000
Hawaii	$100,000
Idaho	$100,000 - $300,000
Illinois	$100,000
Indiana	$100,000
Iowa	$100,000
Kansas	$100,000
Kentucky	$100,000
Louisiana	$100,000
Maine	$100,000
Maryland	$100,000
Massachusetts	$100,000
Michigan	$100,000
Minnesota	$100,000 - $300,000
Mississippi	$100,000
Missouri	$100,000
Montana	$100,000
Nebraska	$100,000
Nevada	$100,000
New Hampshire	$100,000
New Jersey	$100,000 - $500,000
New Mexico	$100,000
New York	$500,000
North Carolina	$300,000
North Dakota	$100,000
Ohio	$100,000
Oklahoma	$300,000
Oregon	$100,000
Pennsylvania	$100,000
Rhode Island	$100,000
South Carolina	$300,000
South Dakota	$100,000
Tennessee	$100,000
Texas	$100,000
Utah	$200,000
Vermont	$100,000
Virginia	$100,000
Washington	$500,000
West Virginia	$100,000
Wisconsin	$300,000
Wyoming	$100,000

INDEX

Italic page numbers indicate figures and tables.

E

F

S

T